Black Regulars
and Militiamen
in the War of 1812

Also by Eric Eugene Johnson

American Prisoners of War Held at Quebec During the War of 1812:
8 June 1813 – 11 December 1814

Ohio and the War of 1812:
A Collection of Lists, Musters and Essays

Ohio's Regulars in the War of 1812

Ohio's Black Soldiers Who Served in the Civil War

American Prisoners of War held in Montreal and Quebec
During the War of 1812

American Prisoners of War Paroled at Dartmouth, Halifax,
Jamaica and Odiham during the War of 1812

Black Regulars in the War of 1812

American Prisoners of War Held at Dartmoor
during the War of 1812

Black Regulars ^*and Militiamen* in the War of 1812

Eric Eugene Johnson

Society of the War of 1812
in the
State of Ohio

HERITAGE BOOKS
2017

HERITAGE BOOKS
AN IMPRINT OF HERITAGE BOOKS, INC.

Books, CDs, and more—Worldwide

For our listing of thousands of titles see our website
at
www.HeritageBooks.com

Published 2017 by
HERITAGE BOOKS, INC.
Publishing Division
5810 Ruatan Street
Berwyn Heights, Md. 20740

Copyright © 2017 Society of the War of 1812 in the State of Ohio

Heritage Books by the Society of the War of 1812 in the State of Ohio:

Transcribed by Harrison Scott Baker

American Prisoners of War Held at Bermuda, Cape of Good Hope and Jamaica During the War of 1812
American Prisoners of War Held at Barbados, Newfoundland and New Providence During the War of 1812
American Prisoners of War Held at Halifax During the War of 1812, Volume I and II

Transcribed by Eric Eugene Johnson

American Prisoners of War Held at Dartmoor During the War of 1812
American Prisoners of War Held in Montreal and Quebec During the War of 1812
American Prisoners of War Held at Quebec During the War of 1812, 8 June 1813–11 December 1814
American Prisoners of War Paroled at Dartmouth, Halifax, Jamaica and Odiham During the War of 1812
Black Regulars in the War of 1812
Black Regulars and Militiamen in the War of 1812
Ohio and the War of 1812: A Collection of Lists, Musters and Essays
Ohio's Regulars in the War of 1812

All rights reserved. No part of this book may be reproduced or transmitted in any form or by any means, electronic or mechanical, including photocopying, recording or by any information storage and retrieval system without written permission from the author, except for the inclusion of brief quotations in a review.

International Standard Book Numbers
Paperbound: 978-0-7884-5772-2

The Introduction

The Black soldier was a rarity between the Revolutionary War and the Civil War. It is said that approximately 5,000 free Blacks and slaves served in the Continental Army during the Revolution. The Blacks proved their worth, many fought with distinction, and many died for their country.

During the Civil War, the U.S. Congress gave President Abraham Lincoln the authority to enlist Blacks as soldiers under the Militia Act of 1862.[1] 209,145 Black men would serve in the United States Colored Troops and in the United States Navy during this conflict. The Colored Troops would represent one-tenth of the total Union Army's strength during the war, while 40% of the Colored Troops would become casualties, either from the bullet or by disease.

Between these two wars, the Black man would be delegated to serve only as a company cook or a White officer's servant. The U.S. Navy would enlist Blacks on equal footing with the common sailors, however, the petty officer ranks and the officer ranks would still be off-limits to Blacks.

Cracks in this restriction appeared for a short time during the War of 1812. Without proper rules and regulations governing this issue, some commanders in the army did recruit Blacks as soldiers, although the total number of identified men is 455. Louisiana did permit Blacks to serve in its state militia, and 557 known Blacks fought at the Battle of New Orleans in 1815. Another 105 men have been found serving as militiamen, cooks and servants in the militia. There are many more Blacks to be discovered in U.S. Army and militia records.

The army did record, to some extent, on its enlistment rosters whether the soldier was White or Black. The recorded physical description of a soldier also indicated race, but this was not always accurate. The *Register of Enlistments in the U.S. Army, 1798-1914*[2] is an extract of personnel information from the land forces of the United States obtained from documents generated by the U.S. Army. These documents include enlistment records, recruiting reports, discharge records, commissioning records, muster rosters, inspection reports, morning reports, court-martial records, etc.

Prior to the War of 1812 there were Blacks serving as cooks and servants in the army. Black slaves serving as servants usually didn't have surnames, and nicknames were used as their given names, that is, Bob or Bill. In the comments section of the enlisted rosters, it may indicate that Bill was a Negro boy who was a servant for a particular officer while Bob was a Colored cook for a particular regiment.

The records generated during the War of 1812 have great genealogical value because the army recorded the age and place of birth, date and place of enlistment, physical descriptions, and the comment section highlighted the career of a soldier. Two problems exist: one, not all of the information is recorded for each soldier, and two, it is hard to spot a Mulatto (unless identified in a record), especially a very light skin Mulatto.

In the name column of the enlistment record there may be the words "negro," "black," "colored," or "mulatto" under the person's name. Likewise, these words may replace "private" in the rank column. "Colored" is often abbreviated as "Col'd" and Black as "Blk." The comments section also used these words but usually within sentences. Other terms that were used are "Negro boy," "Colored man," and "Blackman."

The army also captured the physical descriptions of a soldier by denoting the color of the eyes, the color of the hair, and the complexion (color of the skin) in the *Register of Enlistments*. During the 1800's, the term 'colored' denoted anyone who wasn't white (Caucasian). In the records of the United States

---

[1] Sander, George P., *The Statues at Large, Treaties and Proclamations of the United States of America*, Volume XII, (Little, Brown and Company: Boston, MA 1863), pp. 597-600, Thirty-seventh Congress, session II, chapter 201, *An act to amend the Act calling forth the Militia to execute the Laws of the Union, suppress Insurrections, and repel Invasions, approved February twenty-eight, seventeen hundred and ninety-five, and the Acts amendatory thereof, and for other Purposes*, section 12 and 13.

[2] *Register of Enlistments in the U.S. Army, 1798-1914*; (National Archives Microfilm Publication M233, 81 rolls); Records of the Adjutant General's Office, 1780's-1917, Record Group 94; National Archives, Washington, D.C.

Colored Troops during the Civil War you will find Hawaiians, Mexicans and Filipinos, among other ethnic groups, serving with the Blacks.

The color of the eyes will not denote race since all races had black eyes including Caucasians. Caucasians will also have red, blue, green, hazel, gray, and other colors for eyes. People of mixed races can also have eye color variants. Most races will have either a dark brown or black hair while Caucasians will have many different hair colors. In the army records, 'curly' will also denote a Colored person. The U.S. Navy enlistment records in the Civil War uses "wool" to identify Black sailor's hair color.

The recording on the complexion of a soldier is the best indicator of race. The color black is rarely used for a Caucasian. The terms used for a Caucasian are light, dark, fair, ruddy, sallow, freckled, flesh, red, sandy or florid. Other terms do exist. The terms used to describe Blacks or Mulattoes are black, brown, chestnut, or yellow. The last three terms usually denote a Mulatto. The term 'yellow' is extremely interesting. In the 1800's, you were either White or Colored. "Yellow" was used to denote a mixed race person who wasn't fully white or fully Black. It did not mean that the person was Asian.

Using the three physical characteristics of a soldier may indicate either a Black or Mulatto soldier. These are:

Eyes	Hair	Complexion
Black	Black	Black
Black	Curly	Black
Black	Black	Yellow
Black	Curly	Yellow
Brown	Brown	Brown

Many Irish, Germans and men from the Mediterranean area of Europe are listed as having black or brown complexion along with black eyes and hair or brown eyes and hair. The place of birth is important to identify these men as Caucasian and not as Colored. However, Portugal and Spain were once slave nations and men identified with black or brown complexion could very well had been freed Blacks.

During the war, the British navy blockaded the coastline of the United States and bottled up most of our naval ships, merchant ships and privateers. The majority of Blacks recruited for the army were unemployed sailors who were sitting idle on the docks of Boston and Philadelphia. Most of these men were foreigners and many were born in the West Indies. Unless these men are listed as "Colored" in the enlistment records, it would be hard to prove that they were Colored simply because many of these men returned to the sea and possibly to their native countries after the war. However, many of them may have eventually settled in the United States and become citizens.

A few of the Black men received land bounties and pensions after the war. In order to receive a land bounty, you had to apply for this benefit and you had to have your discharge papers. Many Blacks did not apply for a land bounty simply because they could not read or write, and others may have lost their discharge papers. Black men who enlisted with the 26th Regiment of U.S. Infantry in Philadelphia never joined the regiment in the field and they were not entitled to land bounties. Army requirements stated that all recruits had to join their regiments in the field in order to qualify for a land bounty. The war ended before these men were sent north from Philadelphia to join their regiment in New York. Some men did receive a land bounty but most had their bounties rejected by the War Department in 1820. Other Black soldiers who joined other regiments in New England did receive land bounties because they were sent from the recruiting depots to their regiments.

John Stagg, in his article on the enlisted men in the United States Army during the War of 1812, estimated that there were between 280 and 370 Blacks in the army.[3] His analysis of the army's *Register of Enlistments* showed that only 0.6% of those men whose skin color was noted had 'black' complexions.

---

[3] Stagg, John C. A., <u>Enlisted Men in the United States Army, 1812-1815: A Preliminary Survey</u>, *The William and Mary Quarterly*, Third Series, Volume XLIII, Number 4, October 1986, pp. 615-645.

There were some men who were identified as "colored men' and their complexion were listed as either yellow or brown. Stagg stated that only 4,063 men had their physical descriptions recorded in the *Register of Enlistments*, which leaves the possibility that many more Blacks can be found who enlisted in the army.

The majority of regiments found to have Blacks in their ranks, had only one or two men. The 26th Regiment of U.S. Infantry had the most Black men but this is not a factor since these men never joined the regiment in the field and they never served as combat soldiers. Most Blacks in this regiment have been identified due to the excellent record keeping of Captain William Bezeau who recruited these Blacks for the 26th Infantry.

This leaves the U.S. Light Artillery, the U.S. Corps of Artillery, and the 11th, 30th and 31st Infantries which enlisted more than five Blacks as possible candidates to have additional Blacks found within their ranks. Many of these Blacks served in the same companies together which may be another indicator that other Blacks will be found.

Every free able-bodied white male citizen

When Congress passed the Militia Act of 1792,[4] it required that "every free able-bodied white male citizen" join his state militia. It is implied that non-whites could not participate in the militia but it left open the possibility that non-whites could join the U.S. Army. On 5 April 1799,[5] the War Department established the requirements for its recruiting service by stating, "natives of good character, are always to be preferred for soldiers. Foreigners of good reputation, for sobriety and honesty, may be enlisted; but Negroes, Mulattoes, or Indians are not to be enlisted."

This new ruling only limited Blacks from being soldiers but they could still serve as cooks and servants. In 1802[6] Congress helped the officers who hired servants, or used their personal slaves as servants, by permitting the army to supply one ration (meal) per day for these individuals. Officers had always been allowed to take a private from within the officer's command to serve as a servant. These privates serving in this capacity were usually called "waiters."

Congress in 1812, when passing legislation to provide for the army, increased support for officer's servants by stating, "that the officers who shall not take waiters from the line of the army, shall receive the pay, clothing and subsistence allowed to a private soldier."[7] This was a big boost for Black servants, for the U.S. Army would now feed, pay and cloth these men on the same level as a private. Servants would now receive two rations per day, the same as provided to the privates.

Legislation in 1814 forbid officers from employing soldiers as servants and stated that the names of the servants must now appear on the muster rolls for each corps.[8] Servants were now full members of the U.S. Army. This legislation was not enforced and the names of most servants, White or Black, continued to be left off most of the muster rolls.

Cracks in these restrictions appeared for a short time during the War of 1812. Congress passed *An Act for Completing the Existing Military Establishment*[9] on 24 December 1811 in which was stated that only "able bodied men" may be recruited in the army. No restrictions for race will appear in any military legislation passed during the War of 1812.

Without proper rules and regulations governing this issue of recruiting Black soldiers, some commanders in the army did recruit Blacks although the total number of known men is now 455. Louisiana did permit free Blacks to serve in the state militia, and 557 Black men fought in the Battle of New Orleans. The total number of Blacks possible serving in the army and the state militias was likely to

---

[4] Peters, Richard, *The Public Statutes at Large of the United States of America*, Volume I, (Charles C. Little and James Brown: Boston, MA 1845), pp.271-274, Second Congress, 1st session, chapter 33, 8 May 1792, *An Act more effectually to provide for the National Defense by establishing a Uniform Militia throughout the United States*, section 1.

[5] *War Department, Rules and Regulations Respecting the Recruiting Service*, April 5, 1799, Article III – Natives of good character, are always to be preferred for soldiers. Foreigners of good reputation, for sobriety and honesty, may be enlisted; but Negroes, Mulattoes, or Indians are not to be enlisted.

[6] Peters, *Public Statutes*, Volume II, (Charles C. Little and James Brown: Boston, MA 1845), pp.132-137, Seventh Congress, 1st session, chapter 9, 16 March 1802, *An Act fixing the Military Peace Establishment of the United States*, section 5.

[7] Peters, *The Public Statutes*, Volume II, (Charles C. Little and James Brown: Boston, MA 1845), pp.784-785, Twelfth Congress, 1st session, chapter 137, 6 Jul 1812, *An Act making further Provision for the Army of the United States, and for other purposes*, section 5.

[8] Peters, *Public Statutes*, Volume III, (Charles C. Little and James Brown: Boston, MA 1846), pp.113-116, Thirteenth Congress, 2nd session, chapter 37, 30 March 1814, *An Act for the better organizing, paying, and supplying the Army of the United States*, section 10.

[9] Peters, *The Public Statutes*, Volume II, (Charles C. Little and James Brown: Boston, MA 1845), pp.669-680, Twelfth Congress, 1st session, chapter 10, 24 December 1811, *An Act for Completing the Existing Military Establishment*, section 2.

be less than 1,500 men. There were maybe another 500 light-skinned Mulattoes in the rest of the military forces.

All Blacks were discharged in May of 1815 regardless of their enlistment obligations. Some of the comments in the *Register of Enlistments* state that Colonel Henry Atkinson of the 6th Regiment of U.S. Infantry issued the discharge order on behalf of the War Department. The author has found no general orders from the Department of War ordering Blacks to be dismissed from the service. Most likely, this may have been a general order issued by the Army of the North in New York.

The Adjutant General's Department of the Department of War did issue a general order on 18 February 1820 stating that "no negro or mulatto will be received as a recruit of the army." [10] This order does not direct officers from discharging Negroes or Mulattoes, only that they can no longer recruit these men. Regardless, this general order ended the Black man's participation as a soldier in the army until the Civil War.

Louisiana's Free Men of Color

Louisiana was the only state which permitted free Blacks to become members of the state militia. This is probably due to the fact that Louisiana was the only state not established under English laws but under the French Napoleonic Code. Louisiana's militia laws were 'grandfathered' so that the state did not have to abide by the Militia Act of 1792 restricting Blacks from serving in the state militia.

A common myth is that Andrew Jackson created the two Black militia battalions that served under him during the Battle of New Orleans. Both battalions had existed before the war. On 21 September 1814 while at his headquarters in Mobile, Mississippi Territory (now Alabama), Jackson issued a proclamation to the 'Free Colored Inhabitants of Louisiana' to join their state militia.[11] On 18 December 1814 while at New Orleans, Jackson issued a broadside calling for free Blacks to join these battalions. Both battalions were under strength and Jackson was able to bring these units up to full strength in time for the Battle of New Orleans. The two battalions were under the commands of Majors Pierre Lacoste and Louis D'Aquin, and they consisted of Black officers and Black enlisted men.

Thomas Moebs in his book, *Black Soldiers – Black Sailors – Black Ink,* lists the men who served in these two Louisiana Free Black battalions.[12] He also lists some of the men who enlisted in the U.S. Army and in the U.S. Navy during the War of 1812.

The Black regiments of New York and Pennsylvania

Both New York City and Philadelphia raised Black regiments during the War of 1812, but these units were not military regiments. These regiments were construction battalions used to create military fortifications around New York City, south of Philadelphia, and at Sackets Harbor, NY.

The New York legislature passed *An Act to authorize the raising of two regiments of Men of Color* on 24 October 1814 to serve for three years or less.[13] Each regiment would have 1,080 men consisting of white officers with free and slave Colored men. The slaves would be entitled to be freed upon discharge.

---

[10] Drum, Richard C. (Brigadier General), *Adjutant General's Department*, Subject Index of the General Orders of the War Department from January 1, 1809 to December 31, 1860, page 122, 18 February 1820, general order, "no negro or mulatto will be received as a recruit of the army."

[11] Wilson, Joseph T., *The Black Phalanx: A History of the Negro Soldiers of the United States in the Wars of 1775-1812, 1861-1865,* (American Publishing Company: Hartford, CT, 1890), Chapter II, The War of 1812, pp. 72-80.

[12] Moebs, Thomas Truxtun, *Black Soldiers – Black Sailors – Black Ink: Research Guide of African-Americans in U.S. Military History, 1512-1900,* (Moebs Publishing Co.: Chesapeake Bay, VA 1994).

[13] Williams, George W., *History of the Negro Race in America from 1619 to 1880,* (G. P. Putnam's Sons: New York, 1883), volume II, chapters 2 and 3, pages 23-27, Negro Troops in the War of 1812 and Negroes in the Navy.

Congressman Henry Martindale of New York said in a speech delivered on the 22 January 1828 before the U.S. House of Representatives that "slaves or negroes who had been slaves were enlisted as soldiers in the war of the Revolution: and I myself saw a battalion of them, as fine martial looking men as I ever saw attached to the Northern army in the last war (1812), on its march from Plattsburg to Sacket's Harbor, where they did service for the country with credit to New York and honor to themselves." [14]

The Pennsylvania regiment was recruited by three Black Philadelphians for the defense of this city. An excerpt from the *Missing Pages in American History* [15] states "armed by the conduct of the foe at Washington and Baltimore, many of the other coast cities began to make preparation for their own protection. In Philadelphia, the Vigilance Committee solicited the aid of Absolem Jones, Richard Allen and James Forten, all Negroes. It was desired that these men should secure the services of members of their own race in erecting defenses about the city. Through their efforts twenty-five hundred black men were gathered in the yard of the State House in August and marched to Grey's Ferry, on the west side of the Schuylkill River, where for two days they were employed in throwing up fortifications, for which they received a vote of thanks, tendered them by the city. Mr. Forten himself worked on these breastworks with twenty of his journeymen. A body of colored troops was organized there at this time and placed under an officer of the United States Army."

British Black regiments

Britain raised the Corps of Colonial Marines during the War of 1812 which included runaway American slaves from the Chesapeake Bay area and later along the Georgia coast. Two battalions of Black marines were created. One battalion of marines served in the Chesapeake Bay area while the other battalion served off the east coast of Florida. Upon discharge at war's end, the northern battalion of 700 men settled in Trinidad while the southern battalion of 300 men stayed in Florida and eventually became a part of the Black Seminoles.

The British also sent three Black West Indian Regiments to Louisiana before the Battle of New Orleans. These were the 1st, 2nd and 5th West India Regiments. In Canada, the 104th Regiment of Foot enlisted Black pioneers. Pioneers were soldiers who were armed with an ax and a shovel. They cleared a path for the regiment in woods or over rough terrain.

The Canadian militia also had a company of Blacks serving along the Niagara frontier.[16] Captain Robert Runchey commanded the Company of Coloured Men in the 1st Regiment of Lincoln Militia of Upper Canada (now Ontario). This company would first serve as infantrymen but would later be formed into the Corps of Artificers in early 1813.

American Service

This book highlights 455 known African Americans who served in the U.S. Army during the War of 1812. Many servants are not listed on the musters rolls of the various regiments as was required by army regulations. Many Mulattoes are hidden in the enlistment records because they are very light skinned and could pass as Caucasian. This leaves the possibility of identifying more Blacks in the future who enlisted in the army during this war. Some of these men may only be identified though family histories and traditions.

---

[14] Wilson, *The Black Phalanx*, (American Publishing Company: Hartford, CT, 1890), Chapter II, The War of 1812, pp. 72-80.

[15] Wilkes, Laura E., *Missing Pages in American History: Revealing the Service of Negroes in the Early Wars in the United States of America, 1641-1815*, (Press of R. L. Pendleton: Washington, DC, 1919), War of 1812, pages 65-66, Philadelphia.

[16] Irving, L. Homfray, *Officers of the British Forces in Canada during the War of 1812*, (Welland Tribune Printers, 1908), page 76, The Upper Canada Militia, Captain Runchey's Company of Coloured Men.

Very few of these men ever saw any type of combat. Of the 455 men, 258 were recruits that never left Philadelphia. Of the remaining 197 men, eighteen were officer's servants which leaves 179 men. Of the fifty-four men who served in the U.S. Light Artillery, the majority of these men served at Fort Independence in Boston Harbor. Apparently, these men were used to free White soldiers for combat. This appears to hold true for the Black men of the 10th Regiment of U.S. Infantry who were stationed at Fort Washington, MD.

Three Blacks died during their enlistment, not from wounds received during battle but from disease. Four men became prisoners of war. One of these men was wounded. Another man was wounded during the Battle of Chippewa and a final man was wounded during one of the battles at Fort Erie. Both of these battles occurred in Ontario, Canada. One Black soldier served with the U.S. naval squadron on Lake Champlain on temporary duty.

Of the seventy-three land bounties issued to Blacks for service during the war, sixty-one of these were for men in the 26th Regiment of U.S. Infantry. These men were recruits and were not entitled to land bounties according to army regulations.[17] Ten of these land bounties were rejected and five were re-issued. The majority of these land bounties were issued after 1850 when the militia was able to apply for land bounties due to War of 1812 service. Three men received pensions for their service. Jordan B. Noble received both a land bounty and a pension due to his service during the Mexican War.

Some commanders were not comfortable having Blacks serving in the U.S. Army. Major General George Izard was in charge of the Northern Army in New York during the last year of the war. He tried to transfer all of the Blacks under his command into a Pioneer Corps, which would do the manual labor for his army. In his letter to the Secretary of War on 3 July 1814,[18] he stated, "there was, some years ago, a regulation of our service, prohibiting the enlistment of negroes and people of colour. I have not heard of its being enforced. Among the New England recruits there have lately been brought hither a number of these people, to the great annoyance of the officers and soldiers here. The latter object to doing duty with them. The Inspector General is now organizing them as a sort of pioneer corps. Shall they be retained and mustered in that capacity?" Apparently this never happened! None of the comments included in each of the men's service records indicates that any of the Colored men were transferred to a Pioneer Corps.

---

[17] Drum, Richard C. (Brigadier General), *Adjutant General's Department*, Subject Index of the General Orders of the War Department from January 1, 1809 to December 31, 1860, page 26, 4 March 1815, general order, Recruits enlisted for the war, and discharged without joining any regiments or corps, will not receive the retained bounty.

[18] *Official Correspondence with the Department of War relative to the Military Operations of the American Army under the Command of Major General Izard of the Northern Frontier of the United States in the Years 1814 and 1815*, (William Fry, Printer: Philadelphia, 1816), pp. 45-46, Letter from Major General Izard to the Secretary at War, 3 July 1814.

The Regiments

10th Regiment of U.S. Infantry
11 January 1812 – 17 May 1815

The 10th Regiment of U.S. Infantry was organized under the Acts of 11 January 1812 and 26 June 1812. Under the Act of 3 March 1815, the regiment was consolidated with the 8th, 36th and 38th Regiments of U.S. Infantry to form the new 6th Regiment of U.S. Infantry on 17 May 1815.

The regiment was raised primarily in North Carolina and enlistments were for five years, eighteen months or 'during the war.' The recruiting headquarters was located in Wilkesboro, North Carolina. The regiment participated in the Battle of Chateauguay, Upper Canada, on 26 October 1813 and in the Battle of La Cole Mill, Lower Canada, on 30 March 1814.

11th Regiment of U.S. Infantry
11 January 1812 – 17 May 1815

The 11th Regiment of U.S. Infantry was organized under the Acts of 11 January 1812 and 26 June 1812. Under the Act of 3 March 1815, the regiment was consolidated with the 25th, 27th, 29th and 37th Regiments of U.S. Infantry to form the 6th Regiment of U.S. Infantry on 17 May 1815.

The regiment was raised in Vermont, New Hampshire and Connecticut. Recruiting headquarters were established in Rutland and Bennington, Vermont, with enlistments or five years, eighteen months or 'during the war.' The 11th Infantry saw action in the following battles: Crystler's Fields, La Cole Mill, Fort Erie, Chippewa, and Lundy's Lane. All of these battles were in Upper Canada.

26th Regiment of U.S. Infantry
30 March 1814 to 17 May 1815

The 26th Regiment of U.S. Infantry was organized from the U.S. Voluntary Corps under the provisions of section twenty-one of the Act of 30 March 1814 as the 48th Regiment of U.S. Infantry. The regiment was re-designated as the 26th Regiment of U.S. Infantry on 12 May 1814 under section 13 of the Act of 30 March 1814. The regiment was consolidated on 17 May 1815 under the Act of 3 March 1815 with the U.S. Regiment of Light Artillery.

The regiment was assigned to be raised in Vermont but it maintained recruiting stations in New England, New York, Philadelphia and Baltimore. The recruiting headquarters was located in Burlington, Vermont. Enlistments were for five years or eighteen months. Armed with rifles, the 26th Infantry participated in the Battles of Fort Erie in August and September of 1814.

Captain William Bezeau was the recruiting officer for the 26th Infantry at Philadelphia. He recruited 258 Blacks between August 1814 and June 1815. The captain also recruited Caucasians which he kept as a separate detachment. His detachments were stationed at Lareretto Barracks, south of Philadelphia in Tinicum Township, Delaware County. The barracks were a part of the Lareretto Quarantine Station which was a hospital treating epidemics both locally and those brought into Philadelphia by ships.

Many of the Blacks were detached to work in the station's hospital which was probably used as a military hospital during the war. None of the Black recruits were sent north to join the regiment in New York. At the war's end, those Blacks who enlisted "during the war" were discharged between 20 and 31 May 1815 while the men who enlisted for five years were released between 1 May and 1 June 1815.

The names of most of the Blacks can be found on one of two descriptive rolls maintained for this detachment. The first descriptive roll was dated 1 April 1815 while the other is dated 25 May 1815. The Caucasians were listed on separate descriptive rolls.

30th Regiment of U.S. Infantry
29 January 1813 to 17 May 1815

The 30th Regiment of U.S. Infantry was organized under the Act of 29 January 1813. Under the Act of 3 March 1815 the regiment was consolidated with the U.S. Regiment of Light Artillery on 17 May 1815.

The recruiting headquarters was located at Burlington, Vermont. Originally a one-year regiment with one-year enlistments, the 30th Infantry was converted to a standard regiment with five years or eighteen months enlistments on 28 January 1814. The regiment saw action at La Cole Mill, Lower Canada, and later at Plattsburg, NY, between 6 and 11 September 1814.

31st Regiment of U.S. Infantry
29 January 1813 to 17 May 1815

The 31st Regiment of U.S. Infantry was organized under the Act of 29 January 1813. Under the Act of 3 March 1815 the regiment was consolidated with the U.S. Regiment of Light Artillery on 17 May 1815.

The recruiting headquarters was located at Woodstock, Vermont. Originally a one-year regiment with one-year enlistments, the 31st Infantry was converted to a standard regiment with five years or eighteen months enlistments on 28 January 1814. The regiment saw action at Chateauguay and La Cole Mill in Lower Canada, and at Plattsburg, NY.

Regiment of U.S. Light Artillery
12 April 1808 to 1 June 1821

The Regiment of U.S. Light Artillery was organized under the Act of 12 April 1808 to consists of ten companies. Captain George Peter's company was the only company of this regiment, which prior to the War of 1812, equipped as field artillery. It was mounted as such in 1808 and dismounted in 1809. When the War of 1812 broke out some of the companies were equipped, only for a short time served, as horse artillery and others as field artillery. The Light Artillery served primarily as an elite infantry regiment.

On 17 May 1815, under the Act of 3 March 1815, the 15th, 26th, 30th, 31st, 34th and 45th Regiments of U.S. Infantry were consolidated into this regiment. On 1 June 1821 under the Act of 2 March 1821, the regiment was disbanded and its companies were distributed among the 1st, 2nd, 3rd, and 4th Regiments of U.S. Artillery.

The regiment was raised in the northeastern part of the United States and it had its recruiting headquarters located at Dedham, Massachusetts. Recruitments were for five years or 'during the war.' The Light Artillery participated in the battles at Queenston Heights, Fort George, Stoney Creek and Beaver Dams in Upper Canada, plus French Creek in New York, Crystler's Fields, La Cole, and at Fort Oswego, New York.

The regiment listed the second largest number of Blacks of any U.S. regiment, fifty-four men. The majority of these men were enlisted in Boston by William Campbell and Samuel Washburn. The men served in companies commanded by John Bell, John McIntosh and George Morris. Nearly all of the men served at Fort Independence in Boston Harbor. All of the men were discharged on 31 May 1815 regardless of their enlistment enrollments.

U.S. Corps of Artificers
23 April 1812 to 3 March 1815

The U.S. Corps of Artificers was organized under the Act of 23 April 1812 and the Corps was assigned to the Quartermaster's General Department. The Corps operated with the Army of the North in New York and Vermont. The Corps was discharged under the Act of 3 March 1815.

Alexander Parris was the superintendent of this company size unit. The Corps had an authorized strength of 130 men, made up of both army personnel and civilian workers. They had their own distinct uniform.

The Corps was a construction company which could built and repair supply depots, wagons and boats of the Quartermaster's General Department. The Corps could also make and repair saddles and harness for the department's horses. The blacksmiths could make and repair iron tools and equipment plus horse shoes.

A muster roll of the Corps for May-June 1814, while the corps was stationed at the Burlington Cantonment in Burlington, Vermont, shows the manpower strength of only 73 men.[19] Thirteen men were listed as "Black," all serving as laborers. Some of these Blacks were army soldiers who had been detached from their regiments in order to serve in this Corps.

---

[19] Clark, Byron N., *A List of Pensioners of the War of 1812*, (Research Publication Company: Burlington and Boston, 1904), Payroll of a company of artificers, commanded by Alexander Parris, pp. 129-131.

The Scorecard

This chapter will explain the data fields, abbreviations, terms and phrases used in creating the 'service record' of each individual listed in the following two chapters.

Data Field	Explanation
Rank	The highest known military rank is listed for each soldier.
Regiment	The name of the regiment which the soldier was a member.
Other regiment(s)	If a soldier was transferred to another regiment or regiments, the name of the additional regiment or regiments are listed in this field.
Company	The company commander's name
Age	Age of the soldier at the time of his enlistment
Height	Height of the soldier in feet and inches.
Birth Place	The enlistment rosters list the birth place of a soldier by state or country, county and city.
Trade	Civilian trade of a soldier at the time of enlistment.
Enlistment date	Date that an enlisted man entered service.
Enlistment Place	The place of enlistment by state, county and city.
Enlistment Period	There were four enlistment periods which a soldier could select. All soldiers could choose to re-enlist once their initial enlistment period ended. Those soldiers who enlisted "during the war" were discharged at the end of the War of 1812. 18 Mos = 18 months 1 Yr = 1 year 5 Yrs = 5 years War = "during the war"
By whom	The recruiting officer's name.
Discharged	The date of discharge and location along with other comments.
Died or Killed	Date of death and known location while serving in the army with additional comments.
Pension	I-9999 – Invalid IC-9999 – Invalid's Certificate IF-9999 – Invalid's File IO-9999 – Invalid's Original MC-9999 – Minor's Certificate MO-9999 – Minor's Original SC-9999 – Survivor's Certificate SF-9999 – Survivor's File SO-9999 – Survivor's Original

WC-9999 – Widow's Certificate
WF-9999 – Widow's File
WO-9999 – Widow's Original

Bounty Number   BLW 123456-160-12

BLW = Bounty land warrant number
-160- or -320- = number of acres issued for the warrant
-12 or -14 or -42 or -50 or -55 = Years of the Land Bounty Acts

Comments   Any additional comments for a soldier.

Bounty or land bounty   Regular soldiers were entitled to either 160 or 320 aces of free land for their service during the War of 1812. The heirs of the soldiers, who were killed or who had died in service, were also entitled to bounties.

Descriptive Roll   Each company maintained a Descriptive Roll listing every man in the company, his age, height, weight, color of eyes and complexion, where born, where enlisted, the name of the officer who enlisted him, enlistment date, length of enlistment, and bonus amounts that were paid and what was due. These reports could also include a list of clothing and other supplies that were issued to the soldiers.

Double Bounty   Soldiers who enlisted or re-enlisted on or after 1 February 1814 were entitled to 320 acres of bounty land instead of 160 acres.

Pioneer   A pioneer was a soldier who was delegated to clear a path for a regiment, normally in a wooded area. These soldiers wore a leather apron and used axes and shovels to clear a road.

Recruit   A private still at a recruiting headquarters who had not been assigned to a company and who had not been assigned to his regiment in the field.

Servant   A civilian or slave who served the needs of an officer. This person maintained the household (tent, room or apartment) of an officer and might also perform washing and cooking duties.

Service Record   A service record was any document found in the *Register of Enlistments* which highlighted the service of a soldier.

Surgeon's Certificate of Disability   This was a medical discharge given to a soldier by a regimental surgeon.

Waiter   A waiter was a soldier taken from an officer's command who performed the duties of a servant.

Standard U.S. Postal Service abbreviations are used for U.S. states plus
  LC = Lower Canada (now Quebec)
  UC = Upper Canada (now Ontario)
  NS = Nova Scotia

Heirs obtained half pay for five years in lieu of military bounty land
   Early in the war, the heirs of soldiers who had died (or were killed) during the war and who had enlisted for one-year or 18-months, could elect to receive the soldiers' half-month pay for five years or receive 160 acres of land. This was changed early in the war so that the heirs only received the half pay. The heirs of soldiers who enlisted for five years or during the war always received either 160 or 320 acres of land. 320 acres of land was issued to soldiers who enlisted or re-enlisted after 1 February 1814.

Land bounty to "name of heirs" heirs at law of "name of soldier"
   This phase lists the name(s) of the heir or heirs by law who received the land bounty of a deceased soldier.

- In memory of those who did not return -

The Honored Dead
Who died during the War of 1812

David Davis
Aaron Forman
James Gomaus
Charles Icard
David James
Henry Jones
John Moore
Warner Wallace
Philip Winsell

- Those who die in service to the United States should not be forgotten –

Soldiers in the U.S. Army

-----, Alfred - Waiter - 2nd US Rifles - Company: Benjamin Desha - Enlistment date: 1 Jul 1814 - Listed as a "Mulatto" in his service record; waiter to First Lieutenant John Heddelson.

-----, Andrey - Servant - General Staff - Company: James Hamilton - Private servant to Captain James Hamilton, major assistant inspector general; listed on the payroll report of 31 Jul 1814.

-----, Bill - Waiter - US Quartermaster Department - Company: Nehemiah Baden - Listed as a "Negro boy" in his service record; private waiter to Captain Gustavus Harrison, assistant deputy quartermaster general, Washington, DC.

-----, Bob - Waiter - US Quartermaster Department - Company: Nehemiah Baden - Listed as a "Negro boy" in his service record; private waiter to Major Marstella, Washington, DC (probably Ferdinand Marsteller, assistant deputy quartermaster general).

-----, David - Servant - General Staff - Company: Alexander Macomb - Private servant to Major General Alexander Macomb; listed on the payroll report of 31 Jul 1814.

-----, Edward - Servant - 2nd US Light Dragoons - Company: George Haig - Listed on the Muster Roll of 30 Jun 1814.

-----, Henry - Servant - 2nd US Light Dragoons - Company: George Haig - Listed on the Muster Roll of 30 Jun 1814.

-----, Isaac - Servant - 2nd US Light Dragoons - Company: George Haig - Listed on the Muster Roll of 30 Jun 1814.

-----, James - Waiter - Medical Department – Listed as a "Negro boy"; waiter to Hospital Surgeon's Mate W. Jones, U.S. Hospital, Greenleaf Point, Washington, DC.

-----, Lewis - Waiter - US Ordnance Department - Company: Nehemiah Baden – Listed as a "Negro boy" at Washington, DC, in First Lieutenant Nehemiah Baden's Detachment serving as a private waiter.

-----, Moses - Servant - 2nd US Light Dragoons - Company: George Haig - Listed on the Muster Roll of 30 Jun 1814.

-----, Nace - Waiter - US Ordnance Department - Company: Nehemiah Baden - Listed as a "Negro boy" in his service record; private waiter to First Lieutenant Nehemiah Baden, Assistant Deputy Commissary of Ordnance at Washington, DC.

-----, Reuben - Waiter - US Ordnance Department - Company: Nehemiah Baden - Listed as a "Negro boy" in his service record; private waiter to Captain Morton (probably Captain John Morton, Deputy Commissary of Ordnance).

-----, Robert - Waiter - Unknown rank- Enlistment date: 8 Jun 1814 - Listed as a "Negro boy" in his service record; private waiter in Washington, DC.

-----, Shadrach - Waiter - US Ordnance Department - Company: Nehemiah Baden - Listed as a "Negro boy" in his service record; private waiter to First Lieutenant Nehemiah Baden, Assistant Deputy Commissary of Ordnance at Washington, DC.

Africanus, Major - Servant - 24th US Infantry - Company: Robert Desha - Private servant of First Lieutenant Wyly Martin (probably Black due to his surname).

Alarkin – see Manuel A. Larkin

Aldridge, John - Recruit - 26th US Infantry - Recruiting Detachment: William Bezeau - Age: 22 - Height: 5' 7" - Eyes: Black - Hair: Curly - Complexion: Chestnut - Born: San Domingo (Haiti) - Trade: Laborer - Enlistment date: 9 Jan 1815 - Place: Philadelphia - Period: War - Enlisted by whom: William Bezeau - Pension: Land bounty to Betty Aldridge, sister and only heir at law of John Aldridge; he died before 21 Jun 1819 - BLW 804-320-12 - Listed on the Descriptive Roll of Colored Men, 1 Apr 1815; discharged on 20 Mar 1815.

Alexander, John - Recruit - 26th US Infantry - Recruiting Detachment: William Bezeau - Age: 23 - Height: 6' - Eyes: Black - Hair: Curly - Complexion: Black or Chestnut - Born: Pennsylvania - Trade: Laborer - Enlistment date: 12 Nov 1812 - Place: Philadelphia - Period: 5 Yrs - Enlisted by whom: William Bezeau - Listed as a "Negro man" in his service record; discharged at Philadelphia on 1 May 1815.

Alfred, John - Private - 30th US Infantry - Company: Daniel Farrington - Age: 20 - Height: 5' 11" - Eyes: Black - Hair: Black - Complexion: Black - Born: Sheldon, VT - Trade: Farmer - Enlistment date: 24 Mar 1814 - Place: Plattsburg, NY or Swanton, VT - Period: War - Enlisted by whom: Simeon Wright - BLW 7837-160-42 - Discharged at Plattsburg or Champlain Station, NY, on 17 Jun 1815.

Allen, George - Recruit - 26th US Infantry - Recruiting Detachment: William Bezeau - Age: 16 - Height: 5' - Eyes: Black - Hair: Black - Complexion: Black - Born: Pennsylvania - Trade: Farmer - Enlistment date: 9 Oct 1814 - Place: Philadelphia - Period: 5 Yrs - Enlisted by whom: William Bezeau - Listed as a "Colored man" in his service record; deserted on 18 Oct 1814.

Allen, James - Recruit - 26th US Infantry - Recruiting Detachment: William Bezeau - Age: 22 - Height: 5' 8" - Eyes: Black - Hair: Black or Brown - Complexion: Brown - Born: Philadelphia - Trade: Laborer - Enlistment date: 21 Sep 1814 - Place: Philadelphia - Period: 5 Yrs - Enlisted by whom: William Bezeau - Listed as a "Negro man" in his service record; discharged on 16 May 1815.

Allen, Peter - Recruit - 26th US Infantry - Recruiting Detachment: William Bezeau - Age: 23 - Height: 5' 9" - Eyes: Black - Hair: Curly - Complexion: Chestnut - Born: Pennsylvania - Trade: Farmer - Enlistment date: 11 Jan 1815 - Place: Philadelphia - Period: War - Enlisted by whom: William Bezeau - BLW 830-320-14 Cancelled - Listed on the Descriptive Roll of Colored Men, 1 Apr 1815.

Allen, William - Recruit - 26th US Infantry - Recruiting Detachment: William Bezeau - Age: 21 - Height: 5' 9" - Eyes: Black - Hair: Black - Complexion: Black - Born: Delaware - Trade: Laborer - Enlistment date: 5 Nov 1814 - Place: Philadelphia - Period: War - Enlisted by whom: William Bezeau - BLW 7212-160-12 - Listed as a "Colored man" in his service record; discharged at Philadelphia on 20 Mar 1815.

Alley, William - Recruit - 26th US Infantry - Recruiting Detachment: William Bezeau - Age: 28 - Height: 5' 10" - Eyes: Black - Hair: Curly - Complexion: Brown - Born: Georgia - Trade: Farmer - Enlistment date: 6 Jan 1815 - Place: Philadelphia - Period: War - Enlisted by whom: William Bezeau - Listed on the Descriptive Roll of Colored Men, 1 Apr 1815.

Anderson, Joseph - Recruit - 26th US Infantry - Recruiting Detachment: William Bezeau - Age: 21 - Height: 5' 4" - Eyes: Black - Hair: Curly - Complexion: Black - Born: Louisiana - Trade: Seaman - Enlistment date: 12 Jan 1815 - Place: Philadelphia - Period: War - Enlisted by whom: William Bezeau - Listed on the Descriptive Roll of Colored Men, 1 Apr 1815.

Anderson, Samuel - Recruit - 26th US Infantry - Recruiting Detachment: William Bezeau - Age: 20 - Height: 5' 5" - Eyes: Black - Hair: Black - Complexion: Black - Born: Virginia - Trade: Laborer - Enlistment date: 5 Sep 1814 - Place: Philadelphia - Period: 5 Yrs - Enlisted by whom: William Bezeau - Listed as a "Colored man" in his service record; discharged at Philadelphia on 17 May 1815.

Attire, Peter - Recruit - 26th US Infantry - Recruiting Detachment: William Bezeau - Age: 19 - Height: 5' 6" - Eyes: Black - Hair: Curly - Complexion: Black - Born: Maryland - Trade: Farmer - Enlistment date: 2 Jan 1815 - Place: Philadelphia - Period: War - Enlisted by whom: William Bezeau - Listed on the Descriptive Roll of Colored Men, 1 Apr 1815; deserted on 18 Jan 1815.

Baldwin, Cyrus - Recruit - 26th US Infantry - Recruiting Detachment: William Bezeau - Age: 24 - Height: 5' 9" - Eyes: Black - Hair: Black - Complexion: Black - Born: Pennsylvania - Trade: Laborer - Enlistment date: 10 Oct 1814 - Place: Philadelphia - Period: War - Enlisted by whom: William Bezeau - BLW 7183-160-12 - Listed as a "Colored man" in his service record; discharged at Philadelphia on 20 Mar 1815.

Baptist, John - Laborer - Corps of Artificers - Company: Alexander Parris - Listed as "Black" in *A List of Pensioners of the War of 1812*.

Baptiste, John Delaurier - Recruit - 26th US Infantry - Recruiting Detachment: William Bezeau - Age: 28 - Height: 5' 2" - Eyes: Black - Hair: Curly - Complexion: Black - Born: Africa - Trade: Hatter - Enlistment date: 1 Jan 1815 - Place: Philadelphia - Period: War - Enlisted by whom: William Bezeau - BLW 534-320-14 - Listed on the Descriptive Roll of Colored Men, 1 Apr 1815; discharged at Philadelphia on 20 Mar 1815.

Barager, Francis (Barragher) - Recruit - 26th US Infantry - Recruiting Detachment: William Bezeau - Age: 39 - Height: 5' 6" - Eyes: Hazel - Hair: Black - Complexion: Yellow - Born: New Jersey - Trade: Laborer - Enlistment date: 10 Dec 1814 - Place: Philadelphia - Period: War - Enlisted by whom: William Bezeau - Listed as "Colored" in his service record; discharged at Philadelphia on 20 Mar 1815.

Barber, James - Private - US Light Artillery - Company: George Morris - Age: 40 - Height: 5' 4 1/2" - Eyes: Black - Hair: Black - Complexion: Black - Born: New York, NY - Trade: Laborer - Enlistment date: 7 Oct 1814 - Place: Boston - Period: War - Enlisted by whom: William Campbell - Discharged on 31 Mar 1815.

Barkess – see Jacob Burkess

Barkley, Benjamin (Barclay) - Recruit - 26th US Infantry - Recruiting Detachment: William Bezeau - Age: 23 - Height: 5' 7 1/2" - Eyes: Black - Hair: Black - Complexion: Yellow - Born: Delaware - Trade: Laborer - Enlistment date: 9 Oct 1814 - Place: Philadelphia - Period: 5 Yrs - Enlisted by whom: William Bezeau - Listed as "Col'd" in his service record.

Barnwell, George - Private - 23rd US Infantry - Company: Azariah Odell - Other regiment: 2nd US Infantry - Age: 20 - Height: 5' 7" - Eyes: Black - Hair: Black - Complexion: Black - Born: New

Orleans - Trade: Sailor - Enlistment date: 6 Sep 1814 - Place: Utica, NY - Period: War - Enlisted by whom: Alphonso Wetmore - Transferred to Captain Peter Van Buren's Company, 2nd US Infantry on 30 Apr 1815; deserted from Sackets Harbor, NY, on 27 Feb 1815.

Bean, Peter - Recruit - 26th US Infantry - Recruiting Detachment: William Bezeau - Age: 23 - Height: 5' 3" - Eyes: Brown - Hair: Curly - Complexion: Yellow - Born: Pennsylvania - Trade: Laborer - Enlistment date: 7 Nov 1814 - Place: Philadelphia - Period: 5 Yrs - Enlisted by whom: William Bezeau - Listed as "Col'd" in his service record; discharged on 20 May 1815.

Besenti, Antonio - Private - 43rd US Infantry - Company: Theodore Gourdin - Age: 23 - Height: 5' 3" - Eyes: Black - Hair: Black - Complexion: Dark - Born: San Domingo (Haiti) - Trade: Sailor - Enlistment date: 30 Mar 1814 - Place: Raleigh, NC - Period: War - Discharged at Georgetown, SC, on 27 May 1815.

Bey, Levi - Private - US Light Artillery - Company: John Bell - Age: 21 - Height: 5' 2 3/4" - Eyes: Black - Hair: Black - Complexion: Black - Born: Suffield, CT - Trade: Mariner - Enlistment date: 28 Sep 1814 - Period: War - Enlisted by whom: William Campbell - Discharged on 31 Mar 1815.

Blackford, Isaac - Recruit - 26th US Infantry - Recruiting Detachment: William Bezeau - Age: 26 - Height: 5' 7" - Eyes: Black - Hair: Curly - Complexion: Black - Born: Pennsylvania - Trade: Laborer - Enlistment date: 15 Oct 1814 - Place: Philadelphia - Period: 5 Yrs - Enlisted by whom: William Bezeau - Listed as "Colored" in his service record; discharged at Philadelphia on 23 Mar 1815.

Blackston, David - Recruit - 26th US Infantry - Recruiting Detachment: William Bezeau - Age: 23 - Height: 5' 5" - Eyes: Black - Hair: Curly - Complexion: Black or Chestnut - Born: Delaware or Milford, PA - Trade: Laborer - Enlistment date: 13 Oct 1814 - Place: Philadelphia - Period: 5 Yrs - Enlisted by whom: William Bezeau - Listed as a "Negro" in his service record; discharged at Province Island Barracks, PA, on 29 Feb 1815, Surgeon's Certificate for Disability.

Bladen – Cyrus Baldwin

Blake, William - Recruit - 26th US Infantry - Recruiting Detachment: William Bezeau - Age: 23 - Height: 5' 7" - Eyes: Black - Hair: Black - Complexion: Black - Born: Pennsylvania - Trade: Laborer - Enlistment date: 5 Nov 1814 - Place: Philadelphia - Period: War - Enlisted by whom: William Bezeau - Listed as "Col'd" in his service record.

Bolton Jr., George - Private - 34th US Infantry - Company: Isaac Carter - Age: 27 - Height: 6' 3/4" - Eyes: Grey - Hair: Black - Complexion: Black - Born: Augusta, ME - Trade: Farmer - Enlistment date: 25 Mar 1814 - Place: Portland, ME - Period: War - Enlisted by whom: William Springer - Deserted at Plattsburg, NY, on 8 Sep 1814.

Bonner, Joseph - Private - 16th US Infantry - Company: Thomas McMahon - Other regiment: 2nd US Infantry - Age: 27 - Height: 5' 2 1/2" - Eyes: Black - Hair: Black - Complexion: Dark or Black - Born: Lavaurette, France - Trade: Paver - Enlistment date: 27 Sep 1813 - Place: Little York, PA - Period: 5 Yrs - Enlisted by whom: Samuel Wigley - Discharged at Sackets Harbor, NY, on 27 Sep 1818.

Bosler, John - Recruit Sergeant - 26th US Infantry - Recruiting Detachment: William Bezeau - Age: 40 - Height: 5' 10" - Born: Pennsylvania - Enlistment date: 2 Sep 1814 - Place: Philadelphia - Period: War - Enlisted by whom: William Bezeau - Listed as "Colored" in his service record.

Bowen, John - Private - US Light Artillery - Company: George Morris - Age: 27 - Height: 5' 5" - Eyes: Black - Hair: Black - Complexion: Black - Born: North Hampton, MA or Greenbush, NY - Trade: Farmer - Enlistment date: 6 Oct 1814 - Place: Boston - Period: War - Enlisted by whom: William Campbell - Discharged on 31 Mar 1815.

Bowlin, Richard - Artificer - US Ordnance Department - Company: Robert Richardson - Age: 22 - Height: 6' 1" - Eyes: Yellow - Hair: Black - Complexion: Yellow - Born: Shippensburg, PA - Trade: Laborer - Enlistment date: 10 Feb 1815 - Place: Franklinton, OH - Period: 5 Yrs - Enlisted by whom: Robert Richardson – Discharged on 30 Sep 1816 on Surgeon's Certificate of Disability – Pension: 10098.

Boyington, Richard - Waiter - 11th US Infantry - Company: Staff - Other regiment: 4th US Infantry - Age: 16 - Height: 5' 6" - Eyes: Black - Hair: Black - Complexion: not stated - Born: Vermont - Enlistment date: 25 Jun 1812 - Period: 5 Yrs - Enlisted by whom: Malachi Corning - BLW 15954-160-12 - Listed as "Black" in his service records; waiter to Colonel Henry Atkinson; discharged at Philadelphia on 15 May 1815, under an order from the War Department directing all soldiers of color should be discharged.

Bracken, Hugh - Recruit - 26th US Infantry - Recruiting Detachment: William Bezeau - Age: 27 - Height: 5' 9 1/2" - Eyes: Blue - Hair: Sandy - Complexion: Light - Born: Ireland - Trade: Tobacconist - Enlistment date: 2 Jul 1814 - Place: Philadelphia - Period: War - Enlisted by whom: William Bezeau - Listed as "Colored" with a question mark in his service record; deserted on 24 Jul 1814.

Bradish, William - Private - 31st US Infantry - Company: Andrew Arnolds - Age: 25 - Height: 5' 8 1/2" - Eyes: Black - Hair: Black - Complexion: Black - Born: Litchfield, NH - Trade: Farmer - Enlistment date: 3 Mar 1814 - Place: Montpelier, VT - Period: War - Enlisted by whom: John Hatch - Discharged at Plattsburg, NY, on 6 Jun 1815.

Braho, Joseph - Private - 8th US Infantry - Company: Charles Crawford - Age: 22 - Height: 5' 6" - Eyes: Black - Hair: Black - Complexion: Black - Born: Mexico - Trade: Farmer - Enlistment date: 19 Jan 1814 - Place: Point Petre, GA - Period: 5 Yrs - Enlisted by whom: James Black - Deserted on 22 Feb 1815.

Bridget, Samuel - Private - 26th US Infantry - Recruiting Detachment: William Bezeau - Age: 28 - Height: 5' 4 1/2" - Eyes: Black - Hair: Black - Complexion: Brown - Born: Pennsylvania - Trade: Barber - Enlistment date: 11 Nov 1814 - Place: Philadelphia - Period: 5 Yrs - Enlisted by whom: William Bezeau - Listed as "Col'd" in his service record; discharged at Philadelphia on 17 May 1815.

Broadwell, John - Private - 30th US Infantry - Company: Gideon Spencer - Age: 18 - Height: 5' 8" - Eyes: Black - Hair: Curly - Complexion: Black - Born: New York - Trade: Farmer - Enlistment date: 22 Mar 1814 - Period: War - Enlisted by whom: William Barny - On duty with the 15th Infantry as a waiter.

Brown, Francis - Private - US Light Artillery - Company: John Bell - Age: 24 - Height: 5' 5" - Eyes: Black - Hair: Black - Complexion: Black - Born: Providence, RI - Enlistment date: 22 Aug 1814 - Period: War - Enlisted by whom: William Campbell.

Brown, George - Recruit - 26th US Infantry - Recruiting Detachment: William Bezeau - Enlistment date: 6 Dec 1814 - Period: War - Listed as "Colored" in his service record.

Brown, George - Recruit - 26th US Infantry - Recruiting Detachment: William Bezeau - Age: 25 - Height: 5' 6" - Eyes: Black - Hair: Curly - Complexion: Black - Born: Pennsylvania - Trade: Laborer - Enlistment date: 4 Dec 1814 - Place: Philadelphia - Period: 5 Yrs - Enlisted by whom: William Bezeau - Listed as a "Negro" in his service record; discharged at Philadelphia on 20 May 1815.

Brown, George - Recruit - 26th US Infantry - Recruiting Detachment: William Bezeau - Age: 25 - Height: 5' 7" - Eyes: Black - Hair: Curly - Complexion: Black - Born: Delaware - Trade: Laborer - Enlistment date: 2 Dec 1814 - Place: Philadelphia - Period: 5 Yrs - Enlisted by whom: William Bezeau - Listed as a "Negro" in his service record; discharged at Philadelphia on 29 May 1815.

Brown, James - Private - 1st US Infantry - Company: William Whistler - Enlistment date: 17 Nov 1812 - Place: Erie, PA - Pension: WO-285 Rejected: wife Elizabeth Dorsey - Discharged on 31 Jan 1813; listed as "Colored" in the widow's pension application; died in Aug 1857 in Erie, PA.

Brown, Thomas - Recruit - 26th US Infantry - Recruiting Detachment: William Bezeau - Age: 24 - Height: 5' 8" - Eyes: Black - Hair: Curly - Complexion: Chestnut - Born: Maryland - Trade: Laborer - Enlistment date: 8 Oct 1814 - Place: Philadelphia - Period: War - Enlisted by whom: William Bezeau - BLW 25756-160-12 - Listed as "Col'd" in his service record; discharged at Philadelphia on 23 Mar 1815.

Brown, William - Private - US Light Artillery - Company: John Bell - Age: 35 - Height: 5' 7" - Eyes: Black - Hair: Black - Complexion: Black - Born: St. Croix, Danish West Indies - Trade: Mariner - Enlistment date: 4 Oct 1814 - Place: Boston - Period: War - Enlisted by whom: William Campbell - Discharged on 31 Mar 1815.

Buck, William - Recruit - 26th US Infantry - Recruiting Detachment: William Bezeau - Age: 31 - Height: 5' 5" - Eyes: Black - Hair: Black - Complexion: Dark - Born: Pennsylvania - Trade: Laborer - Enlistment date: 21 Sep 1814 - Place: Philadelphia - Period: War - Enlisted by whom: William Bezeau - BLW 7181-160-12 - Listed as "Col'd" in his service record; discharged at Philadelphia on 23 Mar 1815.

Burd, John - Private - 26th US Infantry - Recruiting Detachment: William Bezeau - Enlistment date: 26 Oct 1814 - Place: Philadelphia - Period: 5 Yrs - Discharged at Philadelphia on 18 May 1815.

Burk, William - Recruit - 26th US Infantry - Recruiting Detachment: William Bezeau - Enlistment date: 7 Oct 1814 - Period: War - Listed as "Col'd" in his service record.

Burkess, Jacob - Recruit - 26th US Infantry - Recruiting Detachment: William Bezeau - Age: 24 - Height: 5' 7 1/2" - Eyes: Grey - Hair: Black - Complexion: Sallow - Born: Pennsylvania - Trade: Blacksmith - Enlistment date: 30 Sep 1814 - Place: Philadelphia - Period: 5 Yrs - Enlisted by whom: William Bezeau - Listed as a "Colored man" in his service record; discharged at Philadelphia on 16 May 1815.

Burkess, William - Recruit - 26th US Infantry - Recruiting Detachment: William Bezeau - Age: 21 - Height: 5' 6" - Eyes: Black - Hair: Black - Complexion: Black - Born: Pennsylvania - Trade: Laborer - Enlistment date: 7 Oct 1814 - Place: Philadelphia - Period: War - Enlisted by whom: William Bezeau - Listed as "Col'd" in his service record; deserted on 15 Oct 1814.

Burns, Charles - Private - US Light Artillery - Age: 24 - Height: 5' 3 1/2" - Eyes: Black - Hair: Black - Complexion: Black - Born: Boston - Trade: Rope maker - Enlistment date: 15 Jul 1814 - Place: Boston - Period: War - Enlisted by whom: Samuel Washburn - Listed as a "Colored man" in his service record; dishonorably discharged at Plattsburg, NY, on 31 May 1815 due to desertions.

Burr, William - Private - 37th US Infantry - Company: Stephen Tilden - Age: 35 - Height: 5' 4" - Eyes: Grey - Hair: Black - Complexion: Black - Born: Greenwich, NJ - Trade: Farmer - Enlistment date: 13 May 1814 - Place: Hartford, CT - Period: War - Enlisted by whom: Daniel Bicknell - Discharged at New London, CT, on 10 May 1815.

Butler, Stephen - Private - US Light Artillery - Listed as "Col'd" in his service record; court-martialed for desertion.

Butt, Thomas - Private - 10th US Infantry - Company: Emanuel Leight - Age: 38 - Height: 5' 8" - Eyes: Grey - Hair: Black - Complexion: Black - Born: Orange County, NC - Trade: Carpenter - Enlistment date: 11 May 1814 - Place: Hillsborough, NC - Period: 5 Yrs - Enlisted by whom: Bennett - BLW 26820-160-12 - Discharged at Washington, DC, on 8 Sep 1815; unfit for service.

Calvin, Caleb - Private - 15th US Infantry - Company: Joseph Barton - Age: 30 - Height: 5' 10 1/2" - Eyes: Black - Hair: Black - Complexion: Yellow - Born: Evesham, NJ - Trade: Laborer - Enlistment date: 6 Mar 1813 - Place: Mount Holly, NJ - Period: 5 Yrs - Enlisted by whom: Joseph Barton - Pension: Land bounty given to Bartholomew Calvin, father & heir at law of Caleb Calvin on 10 Mar 1832 - BLW 26452-160-12 - Discharged at Greenbush, NY, on 1 May 1815.

Campbell, John - Recruit - 26th US Infantry - Recruiting Detachment: William Bezeau - Age: 25 - Height: 5' 8 1/2" - Eyes: Grey - Hair: Black - Complexion: Yellow - Born: Philadelphia - Trade: Tanner - Enlistment date: 13 Sep 1814 - Place: Philadelphia - Period: 5 Yrs - Enlisted by whom: William Bezeau - Listed as a "Black man" in his service record; discharged at Philadelphia on 16 May 1815.

Caze, Shannon Peter (Cage) - Recruit - 26th US Infantry - Recruiting Detachment: William Bezeau - Age: 26 - Height: 5' 8 1/2" - Eyes: Black - Hair: Black - Complexion: Black - Born: San Domingo (Haiti) - Trade: Farmer - Enlistment date: 11 Sep 1814 - Place: Philadelphia - Period: War - Enlisted by whom: William Bezeau - BLW 6440-160-12 - Listed as a "Colored man" in his service record; discharged at Philadelphia on 23 Mar 1815.

Champaigne, Lambert - Private - 19th US Infantry - Company: Joel Collins - Other regiment: 3rd US Infantry - Age: 18 - Height: 5' 6" - Eyes: Black - Hair: Black - Complexion: Black - Born: Detroit, MI - Trade: Laborer - Enlistment date: 6 May 1814 - Place: Detroit, MI - Period: 5 Yrs - Enlisted by whom: John Meldrum - Re-enlisted on 18 Jan 1819.

Chance, Peter - Recruit - 26th US Infantry - Recruiting Detachment: William Bezeau - Age: 27 - Height: 5' 5" - Eyes: Black - Hair: Black - Complexion: Chestnut - Born: Maryland - Trade: Laborer - Enlistment date: 7 Nov 1814 - Place: Philadelphia - Period: 5 Yrs - Enlisted by whom: William Bezeau - Listed as a "Colored man" in his service record; discharged on 18 May 1815.

Charles, Henry - Recruit - 26th US Infantry - Recruiting Detachment: William Bezeau - Age: 22 - Height: 5' - Eyes: Black - Hair: Black - Complexion: Black - Born: Pennsylvania - Trade: Farmer - Enlistment date: 11 Oct 1814 - Place: Philadelphia - Period: 5 Yrs - Enlisted by whom: William Bezeau - Listed as a "Colored man" in his service record; discharged on 20 May 1815.

Chase, Joshua - Black servant - Age: 21 - Born: Baltimore - Prisoner of War interned at Quebec, captured during the Battle of Stoney Point, UC, on 24 Jun 1813, discharged and returned home.

Chestnut, Kinsheon - Private - 10th US Infantry - Company: Robert Mitchell - Other regiment: 8th US Infantry - Age: 18 - Height: 5' 6" - Eyes: Black - Hair: Black - Complexion: Yellow - Born: Sampson County, NC - Trade: Laborer - Enlistment date: 9 Jun 1813 - Place: Duplin County, NC - Period: 5 Yrs - Enlisted by whom: James Hill - Discharged at Fort Crawford, IL, on 9 Jun 1818.

Clinton, Alexander - Recruit - 26th US Infantry - Recruiting Detachment: William Bezeau - Age: 28 - Height: 6' - Eyes: Black - Hair: Curly - Complexion: Black - Born: Virginia - Trade: Farmer - Enlistment date: 4 Jan 1815 - Place: Philadelphia - Period: War - Enlisted by whom: William Bezeau - Listed on the Descriptive Roll of Colored Men, 1 Apr 1815.

Cogler, Josiah - Recruit - 26th US Infantry - Recruiting Detachment: William Bezeau - Age: 27 - Height: 5' 4" - Eyes: Black - Hair: Curly - Complexion: Black - Born: Virginia - Trade: Farmer - Enlistment date: 6 Jan 1815 - Place: Philadelphia - Period: War - Enlisted by whom: William Bezeau - Listed on the Descriptive Roll of Colored Men, 1 Apr 1815.

Congo, Aaron - Recruit - 26th US Infantry - Recruiting Detachment: William Bezeau - Age: 25 - Height: 5' 6" - Eyes: Black - Hair: Black - Complexion: Chestnut - Born: New Jersey - Trade: Laborer - Enlistment date: 16 Sep 1814 - Place: Philadelphia - Period: War - Enlisted by whom: William Bezeau - BLW 10494-160-12 - Listed as a "Colored man" in his service record; discharged at Philadelphia on 20 Mar 1815.

Congo, James - Recruit - 26th US Infantry - Recruiting Detachment: William Bezeau - Age: 26 - Height: 5' - Eyes: Black - Hair: Black - Complexion: Chestnut - Born: New Jersey - Trade: Laborer - Enlistment date: 16 Sep 1814 - Place: Philadelphia - Period: War - Enlisted by whom: William Bezeau - BLW 10495-160-12 - Listed as "Colored" in his service record; discharged at Philadelphia on 23 Mar 1815.

Conner, Hosea - Recruit - 26th US Infantry - Recruiting Detachment: William Bezeau - Age: 27 - Height: 5' 10" - Eyes: Black - Hair: Black - Complexion: Chestnut - Born: Pennsylvania - Trade: Laborer - Enlistment date: 31 Oct 1814 - Place: Philadelphia - Period: 5 Yrs - Enlisted by whom: William Bezeau - Listed as a "Colored man" in his service record; discharged at Philadelphia on 18 May 1815.

Conover, Richard - Recruit - 26th US Infantry - Recruiting Detachment: William Bezeau - Age: 16 - Height: 5' 3 1/2" - Eyes: Hazel - Hair: Black - Complexion: Chestnut - Born: New York - Trade: Laborer - Enlistment date: 5 Oct 1814 - Place: Philadelphia - Period: 5 Yrs - Enlisted by whom: William Bezeau - Listed as "Colored" in his service record; deserted on 15 Nov 1814.

Conrad, James (Conrod) - Recruit Sergeant - 26th US Infantry - Recruiting Detachment: William Bezeau - Age: 33 - Height: 5' 5 3/4" - Eyes: Blue - Hair: Brown - Complexion: Dark - Born: Germany - Trade: Baker - Enlistment date: 17 Aug 1814 - Place: Philadelphia - Period: War - Enlisted by whom: William Bezeau - BLW 12419-160-12 - Listed as a "Colored man" in his service record; discharged at Philadelphia.

Cook, George - Recruit - 26th US Infantry - Recruiting Detachment: William Bezeau - Age: 24 - Height: 5' 10" - Eyes: Black - Hair: Black - Complexion: Yellow - Born: Delaware - Trade: Sailor - Enlistment date: 28 Nov 1814 - Place: Philadelphia - Period: War - Enlisted by whom: William Bezeau - Listed as "Colored" in his service record.

Coomer, Robert (Comer) - Private - US Light Artillery - Company: George Morris - Age: 21 - Height: 5' 5" - Eyes: Black - Hair: Black - Complexion: Black - Born: Jersey - Trade: Mariner - Enlistment date: 6 Oct 1814 - Place: Boston - Period: War - Enlisted by whom: William Campbell - Listed as "Blk" in his service records; deserted on 24 Nov 1814 while on furlough.

Coone, Abraham - Recruit - 26th US Infantry - Recruiting Detachment: William Bezeau - Age: 19 - Height: 5' 2" - Eyes: Black - Hair: Curly - Complexion: Black - Born: Pennsylvania - Trade: Farmer - Enlistment date: 6 Jan 1815 - Place: Philadelphia - Period: War - Enlisted by whom: William Bezeau - Listed on the Descriptive Roll of Colored Men, 1 Apr 1815.

Cooper, John - Recruit - 26th US Infantry - Recruiting Detachment: William Bezeau - Age: 23 - Height: 5' 9" - Eyes: Black - Hair: Black - Complexion: Black or Chestnut - Born: Massachusetts - Trade: Laborer - Enlistment date: 9 Nov 1814 - Place: Philadelphia - Period: War - Enlisted by whom: William Bezeau - BLW 7185-160-12 - Listed as a "Colored man" in his service record; discharged at Philadelphia on 23 Mar 1815.

Cooper, Moses - Recruit - 26th US Infantry - Recruiting Detachment: William Bezeau - Age: 21 - Height: 5' 7" - Eyes: Black - Hair: Curly - Complexion: Brown - Born: Delaware - Trade: Laborer - Enlistment date: 9 Jan 1815 - Place: Philadelphia - Period: War - Enlisted by whom: William Bezeau - Listed as a "Black man" in his service record.

Cox, Joshua (Coxe) - Recruit - 26th US Infantry - Recruiting Detachment: William Bezeau - Age: 21 - Height: 5' 4" - Eyes: Black - Hair: Black - Complexion: Black - Born: Philadelphia - Trade: Farmer - Enlistment date: 13 Sep 1814 - Place: Philadelphia - Period: War - Enlisted by whom: William Bezeau - Listed as a "Colored man" in his service record; discharged at Philadelphia on 20 Mar 1815.

Crane, Asaph - Private - 2nd US Artillery - Company: William Gates - Other regiment: US Light Artillery then U.S. Corps of Artillery - Age: 23 - Height: 5' 11" - Eyes: Brown - Hair: Brown - Complexion: Brown - Born: Canton, MA - Trade: Laborer - Enlistment date: 7 Apr 1812 - Place: Boston - Period: 5 Yrs - Enlisted by whom: Thomas Freeman - Discharged on 6 Apr 1817 and re-enlisted.

Crawford, H. - Private Servant - 2nd Military District - Company: General Staff - Enlistment date: 1 Jun 1814 - Black servant to Brigadier General Thomas Cushing.

Crunkilton, Charles (Crunkitton) - Recruit - 26th US Infantry - Recruiting Detachment: William Bezeau - Age: 24 - Height: 5' 8 1/2" - Eyes: Hazel - Hair: Curly - Complexion: Black - Born: Delaware - Trade: Laborer - Enlistment date: 20 Dec 1814 - Place: Philadelphia - Period: War - Enlisted by whom: William Bezeau - BLW 535-320-14 - Listed as a "Colored man" in his service record; discharged at Philadelphia on 20 Mar 1815.

Cruse, Francis L. - Private - 8th US Infantry - Company: Charles Crawford - Age: 36 - Height: 5' 2 1/2" - Eyes: Black - Hair: Black - Complexion: Black - Born: Havana, Cuba - Trade: Baker - Enlistment date: 3 Dec 1812 - Place: Milledgeville, GA - Period: 5 Yrs - Enlisted by whom: Charles Crawford - Discharged at Fort Hawkins, GA, on 20 Aug 1815 for disability; alias Francis La Cruse.

Culley, Charles - Private - 26th US Infantry - Recruiting Detachment: William Bezeau - Age: 21 - Height: 5' 6" - Eyes: Black - Hair: Curly - Complexion: Black - Born: Delaware - Trade: Farmer - Enlistment date: 4 Feb 1815 - Place: Philadelphia - Period: War - Enlisted by whom: William Bezeau - Listed on the Descriptive Roll of Colored Men, 1 Apr 1815.

Cunnal, William - Recruit - 26th US Infantry - Recruiting Detachment: William Bezeau - Age: 29 -

Height: 5' 9" - Eyes: Black - Hair: Curly - Complexion: Black - Born: Pennsylvania - Trade: Farmer - Enlistment date: 2 Jan 1815 - Place: Philadelphia - Period: War - Enlisted by whom: William Bezeau - Listed on the Descriptive Roll of Colored Men, 1 Apr 1815.

Currell, Bryan - Private - 39th US Infantry - Company: George Hallum - Enlistment date: 20 Dec 1813 - Reported as a Negro; discharged on 19 Dec 1814.

Custis, George - Private - US Light Artillery - Company: John Bell - Age: 35 - Height: 5' 10" - Eyes: Black - Hair: Black - Complexion: Black - Born: Philadelphia - Trade: Sailor - Enlistment date: 10 Oct 1814 - Period: War - Enlisted by whom: William Campbell.

Cutler, Simon - Recruit - 26th US Infantry - Recruiting Detachment: William Bezeau - Age: 20 - Height: 5' 6" - Eyes: Black - Hair: Curly - Complexion: Black - Born: Virginia - Enlistment date: 9 Jan 1815 - Place: Philadelphia - Period: War - Enlisted by whom: William Bezeau - Listed on the Descriptive Roll of Colored Men, 1 Apr 1815.

Cutting, Lewis - Recruit - 26th US Infantry - Recruiting Detachment: William Bezeau - Age: 21 - Height: 5' 3" - Eyes: Black - Hair: Curly - Complexion: Brown - Born: Maryland - Trade: Laborer - Enlistment date: 4 Jan 1815 - Place: Philadelphia - Period: War - Enlisted by whom: William Bezeau - Listed on the Descriptive Roll of Colored Men, 1 Apr 1815.

Dana, Daniel C. - Recruit - 26th US Infantry - Recruiting Detachment: William Bezeau - Age: 19 - Height: 5' 8" - Eyes: Black - Hair: Curly - Complexion: Black - Born: Pennsylvania - Trade: Shoemaker - Enlistment date: 12 Nov 1814 - Place: Philadelphia - Period: War - Enlisted by whom: William Bezeau - Listed as "Col'd" in his service record; deserted on 20 Nov 1814.

Daton, Andrew - Private - 22nd US Infantry - Other regiment: 2nd US Infantry - Age: 21 - Height: 5' 6" - Eyes: Dark - Hair: Dark - Complexion: Dark - Born: New Jersey - Trade: Farmer - Enlistment date: 13 Feb 1815 - Enlisted by whom: Claudius Legrand - Listed as "Colored" in his service record; discharged at Philadelphia on 13 Jun 1815.

Davis, John - Private - 24th US Infantry - Company: James Campbell - Age: 22 - Height: 5' 10" - Eyes: Black - Hair: Black - Complexion: Yellow - Born: Nashville, NC - Trade: Farmer - Enlistment date: 14 Jun 1814 - Place: Tennessee - Period: War - Enlisted by whom: Abraham Britton - Discharged at Camp Mandeville, LA, on 22 Mar 1815.

Dawson, Levi - Recruit - 26th US Infantry - Recruiting Detachment: William Bezeau - Age: 27 - Height: 5' 7" - Eyes: Black - Hair: Curly - Complexion: Chestnut - Born: New Jersey - Trade: Laborer - Enlistment date: 28 Dec 1814 - Place: Philadelphia - Period: War - Enlisted by whom: William Bezeau - Pension: Land bounty cancelled by an order from the War Department on 19 May 1820 - BLW 148-320-14 Cancelled - Listed as "Colored" in his service record; discharged at Philadelphia on 20 Mar 1815.

De Cass John - Private - US Light Artillery - Company: George Morris - Age: 22 - Height: 5' 2 1/2" - Eyes: Black - Hair: Black - Complexion: Black - Born: St. Croix, Danish West Indies - Trade: Seaman - Enlistment date: 4 Aug 1814 - Place: Boston - Period: War - Enlisted by whom: Samuel Washburn - Possible Black, not verified; deserted while on a pass, 6 Nov 1814.

Delany, Mack - Private - 10th US Infantry - Company: George Vashon - Other regiment: 8th US Infantry - Age: 23 - Height: 5' 10 1/2" - Eyes: Grey - Hair: Dark - Complexion: Yellow - Born: Amelia County, VA - Trade: Blacksmith - Enlistment date: 18 Nov 1812 - Place: Halifax County, VA -

Period: 5 Yrs - Enlisted by whom: Emanuel Leight - Discharged on 18 Nov 1817.

Deleva, Antonia - Recruit - 26th US Infantry - Recruiting Detachment: William Bezeau - Age: 34 - Height: 5' 8" - Eyes: Black - Hair: Curly - Complexion: Black - Born: St. Jago, Cuba - Trade: Seaman - Enlistment date: 10 Jan 1815 - Place: Philadelphia - Period: War - Enlisted by whom: William Bezeau - Listed on the Descriptive Roll of Colored Men, 1 Apr 1815.

Delster, James - Recruit - 26th US Infantry - Recruiting Detachment: William Bezeau - Age: 24 - Height: 5' 6" - Eyes: Black - Hair: Curly - Complexion: Black - Born: Cuba - Trade: Seaman - Enlistment date: 2 Jan 1815 - Place: Philadelphia - Period: War - Enlisted by whom: William Bezeau - Pension: Land bounty cancelled by an order from the War Department on 19 May 1820 - BLW 831-320-14 Cancelled - Listed on the Descriptive Roll of Colored Men, 1 Apr 1815.

Dennis, John - Recruit - 26th US Infantry - Recruiting Detachment: William Bezeau - Age: 28 - Height: 5' 10 1/2" - Eyes: Black - Hair: Black - Complexion: Yellow - Born: Pennsylvania - Trade: Fiddler - Enlistment date: 7 Nov 1814 - Place: Philadelphia - Period: 5 Yrs - Enlisted by whom: William Bezeau - Listed as a "Negro" in his service record; discharged at Philadelphia on 18 May 1815.

Derby, Abraham - Laborer - Corps of Artificers - Company: Alexander Parris - Other regiment: 21st Infantry - Enlistment date: 24 Mar 1813 - Period: 18 Mos - Enlisted in the 21st Infantry, attached to the U.S. Corps of Artificers, listed as "Black" in *A List of Pensioners of the War of 1812*.

Derwood, Joshua - Recruit - 26th US Infantry - Recruiting Detachment: William Bezeau - Age: 27 - Height: 5' 10 1/2" - Eyes: Black - Hair: Curly - Complexion: Black - Born: New Jersey - Trade: Farmer - Enlistment date: 1 Feb 1815 - Place: Philadelphia - Period: War - Enlisted by whom: William Bezeau - Listed on the Descriptive Roll of Colored Men, 1 Apr 1815.

Dexter, Jacob - Private - 25th US Infantry - Company: Daniel Ketchum - Height: 5' 9" - Eyes: Black - Hair: Black - Complexion: Black - Trade: Farmer - Enlistment date: 18 Mar 1814 - Place: Windsor, CT - Period: War - Enlisted by whom: Ephraim Shaylor - BLW 25792-160-12 - Listed as a "Colored man" in his service record; wounded in the Battle of Chippewa, UC, 5 Jul 1814; discharged on 28 Mar 1815.

Dickinson, Harry - Private - 30th US Infantry - Company: William Miller - Other regiment: U.S. Corps of Artillery - Age: 21 - Height: 5' - Eyes: Black - Hair: Curly or Black - Complexion: Black - Born: Philadelphia - Trade: Cordwainer - Enlistment date: 8 Apr 1814 - Place: Burlington, VT - Period: War - Enlisted by whom: William Barney.

Domingo, Emanuel - Private - US Light Artillery - Company: George Morris - Age: 26 - Height: 5' 9" - Eyes: Black - Hair: Black - Complexion: Black - Born: St. Croix, Danish West Indies - Trade: Seaman - Enlistment date: 8 Aug 1814 - Place: Boston - Period: War - Enlisted by whom: Samuel Washburn - Also listed as Manuel Domingo; discharged on 31 Mar 1815.

Doras, John - Recruit - US Light Artillery - Age: 19 - Height: 5' 3 3/4" - Born: San Domingo (Haiti) - Enlistment date: 22 Jul 1814 - Place: Boston - Enlisted by whom: Samuel Washburn.

Dorsey, Charles - Recruit - 26th US Infantry - Recruiting Detachment: William Bezeau - Age: 38 - Height: 6' - Eyes: Black - Hair: Curly - Complexion: Chestnut - Born: Pennsylvania - Trade: Farmer - Enlistment date: 10 Feb 1815 - Place: Philadelphia - Period: War - Enlisted by whom: William Bezeau - Pension: Land bounty to Mathew Dorsey, brother & only heir at law of Charles Dorsey; he died before 6 Jul 1819; first land bounty was cancelled by an order from the War

Department on 19 May 1820 - BLW 810-320-14 Cancelled; BLW 1036-320-14 - Listed on the Descriptive Roll of Colored Men, 1 Apr 1815.

Draper, Samuel - Recruit - 26th US Infantry - Recruiting Detachment: William Bezeau - Age: 19 - Height: 5' 6" - Eyes: Black - Hair: Black - Complexion: Black - Born: Maryland - Trade: Laborer - Enlistment date: 11 Oct 1814 - Place: Philadelphia - Period: 5 Yrs - Enlisted by whom: William Bezeau - Listed as "Col'd" in his service record; discharged for being a minor.

Drummond, Levin (also Levi Drummond) - Recruit - 26th US Infantry - Recruiting Detachment: William Bezeau - Age: 25 - Height: 5' 6" - Eyes: Black - Hair: Curly - Complexion: Brown - Born: Virginia - Trade: Farmer - Enlistment date: 17 Nov 1814 - Place: Philadelphia - Period: War - Enlisted by whom: William Bezeau - BLW 7187-160-12 - Listed as "Col'd" in his service record; discharged at Philadelphia on 20 Mar 1815.

Duffin, Edward - Recruit - 26th US Infantry - Recruiting Detachment: William Bezeau - Age: 26 - Height: 5' 8" - Eyes: Black - Hair: Curly - Complexion: Black - Born: Pennsylvania - Trade: Laborer - Enlistment date: 3 Jan 1815 - Place: Philadelphia - Period: War - Enlisted by whom: William Bezeau - Listed on the Descriptive Roll of Colored Men, 1 Apr 1815.

Duke, Simon - Recruit - 26th US Infantry - Recruiting Detachment: William Bezeau - Age: 21 - Height: 5' 4" - Eyes: Black - Hair: Curly - Complexion: Black - Born: Pennsylvania - Trade: Laborer - Enlistment date: 3 Feb 1815 - Place: Philadelphia - Period: War - Enlisted by whom: William Bezeau - Listed on the Descriptive Roll of Colored Men, 1 Apr 1815.

Dunaway, William - Recruit - 26th US Infantry - Recruiting Detachment: William Bezeau - Age: 21 - Height: 5' - Eyes: Black - Hair: Curly - Complexion: Black - Born: Massachusetts - Trade: Laborer - Enlistment date: 11 Oct 1814 - Place: Philadelphia - Period: 5 Yrs - Enlisted by whom: William Bezeau - Listed as "Col'd" in his service record; discharged at Philadelphia on 20 May 1815.

Duperon, Lewis - Private - 44th US Infantry - Company: Anatole Peychaud - Other regiment: 1st US Infantry - Age: 21 - Height: 5' 5" - Eyes: Hazel - Hair: Dark - Complexion: Brown - Born: Jeremy, San Domingo (Haiti) - Trade: Cigar maker - Enlistment date: 28 Nov 1814 - Place: New Orleans - Period: 5 Yrs - Deserted on 30 Oct 1815.

Durang, J. M. F. A. - Recruit - US Light Artillery - Age: 29 - Born: Isle of France (Mauritius) - Enlistment date: 8 Nov 1814 - Place: Providence, RI - Enlisted by whom: Benjamin Robb.

Durker, Alexander - Recruit - 26th US Infantry - Recruiting Detachment: William Bezeau - Age: 27 - Height: 5' 4" - Eyes: Black - Hair: Curly - Complexion: Brown - Born: New York - Trade: Farmer - Enlistment date: 1 Jan 1815 - Place: Philadelphia - Period: War - Enlisted by whom: William Bezeau - Listed on the Descriptive Roll of Colored Men, 1 Apr 1815; deserted on 9 Jan 1815.

Durkham, Vincent - Recruit - 26th US Infantry - Recruiting Detachment: William Bezeau - Age: 31 - Height: 5' 9" - Eyes: Hazel - Hair: Black - Complexion: Yellow - Born: Delaware - Trade: Laborer - Enlistment date: 13 Nov 1814 - Place: Philadelphia - Period: 5 Yrs - Enlisted by whom: William Bezeau - Listed as "Colored" in his service record.

Dury, Joseph - Recruit - 26th US Infantry - Recruiting Detachment: William Bezeau - Age: 27 - Height: 5' 11" - Eyes: Black - Hair: Curly - Complexion: Black - Born: New York - Trade: Laborer - Enlistment date: 1 Feb 1815 - Place: Philadelphia - Period: War - Enlisted by whom: William Bezeau - Deserted on 6 Feb 1815.

Eames, John - Private - US Light Artillery - Company: John Bell - Age: 24 - Height: 5' 2" - Eyes: Black - Hair: Black - Complexion: Black - Born: Newtown or Middleton, NJ - Trade: Farmer - Enlistment date: 4 Nov 1814 - Place: Boston - Period: War - Enlisted by whom: William Campbell - Discharged on 31 Mar 1815.

Ebrian, Charles - Recruit - 26th US Infantry - Recruiting Detachment: William Bezeau - Age: 22 - Height: 5' 11" - Eyes: Black - Hair: Curly - Complexion: Black - Born: Pennsylvania - Trade: Laborer - Enlistment date: 20 Jan 1815 - Place: Philadelphia - Period: War - Enlisted by whom: William Bezeau - Listed on the Descriptive Roll of Colored Men, 1 Apr 1815.

Edderley, William - Recruit - 26th US Infantry - Recruiting Detachment: William Bezeau - Age: 30 - Height: 5' 8" - Eyes: Black - Hair: Curly - Complexion: Black - Born: Pennsylvania - Trade: Laborer - Enlistment date: 3 Jan 1815 - Place: Philadelphia - Period: War - Enlisted by whom: William Bezeau - Listed on the Descriptive Roll of Colored Men, 1 Apr 1815.

Ebant – see George Eliant

Edmunds, Joshua - Recruit - 26th US Infantry - Recruiting Detachment: William Bezeau - Age: 28 - Height: 5' 5" - Eyes: Black - Hair: Curly - Complexion: Black - Born: Pennsylvania - Trade: Farmer - Enlistment date: 16 Jan 1815 - Place: Philadelphia - Period: War - Enlisted by whom: William Bezeau - Listed on the Descriptive Roll of Colored Men, 1 Apr 1815.

Edwards, Simon - Recruit - 26th US Infantry - Recruiting Detachment: William Bezeau - Age: 37 - Height: 5' 9" - Eyes: Black - Hair: Curly - Complexion: Black - Born: Pennsylvania - Trade: Farmer - Enlistment date: 28 Jan 1815 - Place: Philadelphia - Period: War - Enlisted by whom: William Bezeau - Listed on the Descriptive Roll of Colored Men, 1 Apr 1815.

Edwood, James - Recruit - 26th US Infantry - Recruiting Detachment: William Bezeau - Age: 24 - Height: 5' 6" - Eyes: Black - Hair: Curly - Complexion: Black - Born: Kentucky - Trade: Farmer - Enlistment date: 4 Feb 1815 - Place: Philadelphia - Period: War - Enlisted by whom: William Bezeau - Listed on the Descriptive Roll of Colored Men, 1 Apr 1815.

Eliant, George - Recruit - 26th US Infantry - Recruiting Detachment: William Bezeau - Age: 31 - Height: 5' 9" - Eyes: Black - Hair: Curly - Complexion: Brown - Born: Pennsylvania - Trade: Farmer - Enlistment date: 12 Feb 1815 - Place: Philadelphia - Period: War - Enlisted by whom: William Bezeau - Listed on the Descriptive Roll of Colored Men, 1 Apr 1815.

Ellitte, Moses - Recruit - 26th US Infantry - Recruiting Detachment: William Bezeau - Age: 21 - Height: 5' 3" - Eyes: Black - Hair: Curly - Complexion: Chestnut - Born: Delaware - Trade: Farmer - Enlistment date: 5 Jan 1815 - Place: Philadelphia - Period: War - Enlisted by whom: William Bezeau - Listed on the Descriptive Roll of Colored Men, 1 Apr 1815.

Ellsberry, Charles (Ellsbury) - Private - US Light Artillery - Company: George Morris - Age: 35 - Height: 5' 8 1/2" - Eyes: Black - Hair: Black - Complexion: Black - Born: Dover, DE - Trade: Mariner - Enlistment date: 5 Oct 1814 - Place: Boston - Period: 5 Yrs - Enlisted by whom: William Campbell - Listed as "Black" in his service record; discharged on 31 Mar 1815 on account of being a negro and unfit to accompany American soldiers.

Embar, Peter - Recruit - 26th US Infantry - Recruiting Detachment: William Bezeau - Age: 30 - Height: 6' - Eyes: Black - Hair: Curly - Complexion: Black - Born: Pennsylvania - Trade: Farmer - Enlistment date: 10 Jan 1815 - Place: Philadelphia - Period: War - Enlisted by whom: William Bezeau - Listed on the Descriptive Roll of Colored Men, 1 Apr 1815.

Ethington, William - Private - 3rd US Volunteers - Company: Isaac Little - Discharged on 10 Jul 1813 for being a slave.

Eubern, Smith - Recruit - 26th US Infantry - Recruiting Detachment: William Bezeau - Age: 27 - Height: 5' 6" - Eyes: Black - Hair: Curly - Complexion: Brown - Born: Pennsylvania - Trade: Laborer - Enlistment date: 10 Jan 1815 - Place: Philadelphia - Period: War - Enlisted by whom: William Bezeau - Listed on the Descriptive Roll of Colored Men, 1 Apr 1815; deserted on 14 Jan 1815.

Fambert, Lewis - Recruit - 26th US Infantry - Recruiting Detachment: William Bezeau - Age: 22 - Height: 5' 9" - Eyes: Black - Hair: Curly - Complexion: Black - Born: Pennsylvania - Trade: Farmer - Enlistment date: 9 Feb 1815 - Place: Philadelphia - Period: War - Enlisted by whom: William Bezeau - Listed on the Descriptive Roll of Colored Men, 1 Apr 1815; deserted on 15 Feb 1815.

Fanolly, Cato - Private - 5th US Infantry - Age: 24 - Height: 5' 8" - Eyes: Hazel - Hair: Dark - Complexion: Dark - Born: New York, NY - Trade: Waiter - Enlistment date: 17 Aug 1814 - Place: Lancaster, PA - Period: 5 yrs - Discharged on 7 Nov 1817 as a runaway Negro.

Farmer, Cuff - Recruit - 26th US Infantry - Recruiting Detachment: William Bezeau - Age: 36 - Height: 5' 7" - Eyes: Black - Hair: Curly - Complexion: Black - Born: New Jersey - Trade: Farmer - Enlistment date: 28 Nov 1814 - Place: Philadelphia - Period: 5 Yrs - Enlisted by whom: William Bezeau - Listed as "Col'd" in his service record; discharged on 30 Mar 1815.

Fedlow, Edward - Recruit - 26th US Infantry - Recruiting Detachment: William Bezeau - Age: 21 - Height: 5' 7" - Eyes: Black - Hair: Curly - Complexion: Black - Born: New Jersey - Trade: Farmer - Enlistment date: 5 Jan 1815 - Place: Philadelphia - Period: War - Enlisted by whom: William Bezeau.

Fobden, Ezekiel - Recruit - 26th US Infantry - Recruiting Detachment: William Bezeau - Age: 34 - Height: 5' 11" - Eyes: Black - Hair: Curly - Complexion: Black - Born: Pennsylvania - Trade: Farmer - Enlistment date: 8 Feb 1815 - Place: Philadelphia - Period: War - Enlisted by whom: William Bezeau - Pension: Land bounty to Jacob Boys, uncle & only heir of Ezekiel Fobden, deceased; died before 1 Jul 1819; land bounty cancelled by an order from the War Department on 19 May 1820 - BLW 809-320-14 Cancelled - Listed on the Descriptive Roll of Colored Men, 1 Apr 1815.

Fobler, Benjamin - Recruit - 26th US Infantry - Recruiting Detachment: William Bezeau - Age: 30 - Height: 5' 4" - Eyes: Black - Hair: Curly - Complexion: Yellow - Born: Delaware - Trade: Miller - Enlistment date: 15 Nov 1814 - Place: Philadelphia - Period: 5 Yrs - Enlisted by whom: William Bezeau - Pension: Land bounty cancelled by an order from the War Department on 19 May 1820 - BLW 3790-160-12 Cancelled - Listed on the Descriptive Roll of Colored Men, 1 Apr 1815; discharged at Philadelphia on 30 May 1815.

Fobler, John - Recruit - 26th US Infantry - Recruiting Detachment: William Bezeau - Age: 30 - Height: 5' 4" - Born: Delaware - Enlistment date: 15 Nov 1814 - Place: Philadelphia - Enlisted by whom: William Bezeau - Listed as "Col'd" in his service record.

Folbert, Titus - Recruit - 26th US Infantry - Recruiting Detachment: William Bezeau - Age: 28 - Height:

5' 6" - Eyes: Black - Hair: Curly - Complexion: Yellow - Born: Ohio - Trade: Farmer - Enlistment date: 25 Jan 1815 - Place: Philadelphia - Period: War - Enlisted by whom: William Bezeau - Listed on the Descriptive Roll of Colored Men, 1 Apr 1815.

Ford, George - Private - 36th US Infantry - Company: Joseph Hook - Enlistment date: 4 Oct 1813 - Period: 1 Yr - Re-enlisted on 17 Aug 1814 for the war; discharged at Camp Snowden, MD, claimed by his master for being a minor.

Ford, James - Recruit - 26th US Infantry - Recruiting Detachment: William Bezeau - Age: 17 - Height: 5' 5" - Eyes: Black - Hair: Black - Complexion: Yellow - Born: Pennsylvania - Trade: Laborer - Enlistment date: 11 Oct 1814 - Place: Philadelphia - Period: War - Enlisted by whom: William Bezeau - Listed as "Col'd" in his service record; discharged for being a minor.

Forrest, Charles - Recruit - 26th US Infantry - Recruiting Detachment: William Bezeau - Age: 34 - Height: 5' 7" - Eyes: Black - Hair: Curly - Complexion: Black - Born: Pennsylvania - Trade: Laborer - Enlistment date: 11 Feb 1815 - Place: Philadelphia - Period: War - Enlisted by whom: William Bezeau - Listed on the Descriptive Roll of Colored Men, 1 Apr 1815.

Fortland, Isaac - Recruit - 26th US Infantry - Recruiting Detachment: William Bezeau - Age: 29 - Height: 5' 8" - Eyes: Black - Hair: Curly - Complexion: Black - Born: Pennsylvania - Trade: Laborer - Enlistment date: 26 Jan 1815 - Place: Philadelphia - Period: War - Enlisted by whom: William Bezeau - Listed on the Descriptive Roll of Colored Men, 1 Apr 1815.

Foucher, William - Private - 44th US Infantry - Other regiment: 7th US Infantry - Age: 34 - Height: 5' 5" - Born: Cape Francis, San Domingo (Haiti) - Enlistment date: 21 Oct 1813 - Place: Powder Magazine, LA - Transferred to 7th Infantry on 2 Apr 1814.

Francy – see Jacob Freeny

Francis, Joseph - Private - US Light Artillery - Company: George Morris - Age: 23 - Height: 5' 6 1/2" - Eyes: Black - Hair: Black - Complexion: Black - Born: San Salvador, Bahamas - Trade: Barber - Enlistment date: 18 Jul 1814 - Place: Boston - Period: War - Enlisted by whom: Samuel Washburn - Discharged at Plattsburg, NY, on 31 May 1815.

Franklin, Jacob - Recruit - 26th US Infantry - Recruiting Detachment: William Bezeau - Age: 35 - Height: 5' 10" - Eyes: Black - Hair: Curly - Complexion: Brown - Born: Pennsylvania - Trade: Farmer - Enlistment date: 27 Jan 1815 - Place: Philadelphia - Period: War - Enlisted by whom: William Bezeau - Listed on the Descriptive Roll of Colored Men, 1 Apr 1815.

Frederick, Lewis - Private - US Light Artillery - Company: John McIntosh - Age: 25 - Height: 5' 7 1/2" - Eyes: Black - Hair: Black - Complexion: Black - Born: Baltimore - Trade: Mariner - Enlistment date: 14 Jul 1814 - Place: Boston - Period: War - Enlisted by whom: Samuel Washburn - Discharged at Plattsburg, NY, on 31 May 1815.

Freeman, George - Recruit - 26th US Infantry - Recruiting Detachment: William Bezeau - Age: 30 - Height: 5' 8" - Eyes: Black - Hair: Curly - Complexion: Brown - Born: Pennsylvania - Trade: Laborer - Enlistment date: 21 Nov 1814 - Place: Philadelphia - Period: 5 Yrs - Enlisted by whom: William Bezeau - Listed as "Col'd" in his service record; discharged at Philadelphia on 1 May 1815.

Freeman, Joseph - Recruit - 26th US Infantry - Recruiting Detachment: William Bezeau - Age: 26 -

Height: 5' - Eyes: Black - Hair: Black - Complexion: Yellow - Born: New Jersey - Trade: Shoemaker - Enlistment date: 14 Sep 1814 - Place: Philadelphia - Period: 5 Yrs - Enlisted by whom: William Bezeau - Listed as "Col'd" in his service record; discharged at Philadelphia on 17 May 1815.

Freeny, Jacob - Recruit - 26th US Infantry - Recruiting Detachment: William Bezeau - Age: 30 - Height: 5' 8" - Eyes: Black - Hair: Curly - Complexion: Black - Born: Delaware - Trade: Laborer - Enlistment date: 20 Dec 1814 - Place: Philadelphia - Period: War - Enlisted by whom: William Bezeau - Listed as "Col'd" in his service record.

Frey, Michael - Private - 32nd US Infantry - Company: George Goodman - Age: 26 - Height: 5' 6 3/4" - Eyes: Black - Hair: Dark - Complexion: Black - Born: Pennsylvania - Trade: Farmer - Enlistment date: 17 Feb 1814 - Place: Easton, PA - Period: War - Enlisted by whom: Henry Gulick - BLW 4407-160-12 - Discharged at Governor's Island, NY, on 7 May 1815.

Fudy, G. B. - Private Servant - 2nd Military District - Company: General Staff - Enlistment date: 1 Jun 1814 - Listed as "Black" in his service record; servant on the general staff; discharged on 30 Jun 1814.

Fuller, Jacob - Recruit - 26th US Infantry - Recruiting Detachment: William Bezeau - Age: 26 - Height: 5' 5" - Eyes: Black - Hair: Curly - Complexion: Black - Born: Maryland - Trade: Farmer - Enlistment date: 18 Jan 1815 - Place: Philadelphia - Period: War - Enlisted by whom: William Bezeau - Listed on the Descriptive Roll of Colored Men, 1 Apr 1815; deserted on 22 Jan 1815.

Fuller, Quamenaugh - Private - US Light Artillery - Company: John Bell - Age: 37 - Height: 5' 5" - Eyes: Black - Hair: Black - Complexion: Black - Born: Hartford or Lynn, CT - Trade: Laborer - Enlistment date: 13 Aug 1814 - Place: Providence or Dedham, RI - Period: War - BLW 12183-160-12 - Discharged at Boston on 31 Mar 1815.

Fulting, Jeremiah (Futting) - Recruit - 26th US Infantry - Recruiting Detachment: William Bezeau - Age: 34 - Height: 5' 11" - Eyes: Black - Hair: Curly - Complexion: Black - Born: Maryland - Trade: Laborer - Enlistment date: 24 Jan 1815 - Place: Philadelphia - Period: War - Enlisted by whom: William Bezeau - Pension: Land bounty to Jeremiah Hubbard, cousin & only heir at law of Jeremiah Fulting, deceased; first bounty was cancelled by an order from the War Department, 19 May 1820 - BLW 832-320-14 Cancelled; BLW 1039-320-14 - Listed on the Descriptive Roll of Colored Men, 1 Apr 1815.

Gansey, William - Recruit - 26th US Infantry - Recruiting Detachment: William Bezeau - Age: 30 - Height: 5' 8" - Eyes: Black - Hair: Curly - Complexion: Chestnut - Born: Africa - Trade: Laborer - Enlistment date: 16 Dec 1814 - Place: Philadelphia - Period: War - Enlisted by whom: William Bezeau - BLW 7190-160-12 - Listed as "Col'd" in his service record; discharged at Philadelphia on 20 Mar 1815.

Gardiner, Edward - Recruit - 26th US Infantry - Recruiting Detachment: William Bezeau - Age: 29 - Height: 5' 6" - Eyes: Black - Hair: Curly - Complexion: Black - Born: New Jersey - Trade: Laborer - Enlistment date: 21 Sep 1814 - Place: Philadelphia - Period: War - Enlisted by whom: William Bezeau - BLW 3789-160-12 - Listed as "Col'd" in his service record; discharged at Philadelphia on 23 May 1815.

Gardner, William - Private - US Light Artillery - Company: George Morris - Age: 19 - Height: 5' 5 1/2" - Eyes: Black - Hair: Black - Complexion: Black - Born: Boston - Trade: Laborer - Enlistment date:

29 Jul 1814 - Place: Boston - Period: War - Enlisted by whom: Samuel Washburn - Listed as "Black" in his service record; discharged on 31 Mar 1815.

Gardner, William (Gardiner) - Private - US Light Artillery - Company: George Morris - Age: 25 - Height: 5' 11 1/2" - Eyes: Black - Hair: Dark - Complexion: Dark - Born: Londonderry, NH - Trade: Laborer - Enlistment date: 15 Aug 1814 - Place: Dedham, MA - Period: War - Enlisted by whom: William Campbell - Listed as "Black" in his service record.

Garland, William - Recruit - 26th US Infantry - Recruiting Detachment: William Bezeau - Age: 34 - Height: 5' 6" - Eyes: Black - Hair: Curly - Complexion: Chestnut - Born: Pennsylvania - Trade: Laborer - Enlistment date: 28 Jan 1815 - Place: Philadelphia - Period: War - Enlisted by whom: William Bezeau - Listed on the Descriptive Roll of Colored Men, 1 Apr 1815.

Garrish, Jeremiah - Private - US Light Artillery - Company: John Bell - Age: 31 - Height: 5' 3 3/4" - Eyes: Black - Hair: Black or Dark - Complexion: Black or Dark - Born: Hampton or Portsmouth, NH - Trade: Mariner - Enlistment date: 30 Sep 1814 - Place: Boston - Period: 5 Yrs - Enlisted by whom: William Campbell - Discharged on 31 Mar 1815 for being a Negro and not a fit companion for the American soldier.

Gates, Philip - Recruit - 26th US Infantry - Recruiting Detachment: William Bezeau - Age: 37 - Height: 5' 10" - Eyes: Black - Hair: Black - Complexion: Yellow - Born: Pennsylvania - Trade: Weaver - Enlistment date: 23 Oct 1814 - Place: Philadelphia - Period: 5 Yrs - Enlisted by whom: William Bezeau - Listed as "Col'd" in his service record; discharged at Philadelphia on 1 May 1815.

George, William - Recruit - 26th US Infantry - Recruiting Detachment: William Bezeau - Age: 22 - Height: 5' 8" - Eyes: Black - Hair: Black - Complexion: Black - Born: Virginia - Trade: Blacksmith - Enlistment date: 7 Oct 1814 - Place: Philadelphia - Period: War - Enlisted by whom: William Bezeau - BLW 7191-160-12 - Listed as "Col'd" in his service record; discharged at Philadelphia on 20 Mar 1815.

George, William - Recruit - 26th US Infantry - Recruiting Detachment: William Bezeau - Age: 18 - Height: 5' 5" - Eyes: Black - Hair: Curly - Complexion: Black - Born: Africa - Trade: Farmer - Enlistment date: 6 Feb 1815 - Place: Philadelphia - Period: War - Enlisted by whom: William Bezeau - Listed on the Descriptive Roll of Colored Men, 1 Apr 1815.

Gifter, Alexander - Recruit - 26th US Infantry - Recruiting Detachment: William Bezeau - Age: 22 - Height: 5' 7" - Eyes: Black - Hair: Curly - Complexion: Yellow - Born: Georgia - Trade: Farmer - Enlistment date: 7 Feb 1815 - Place: Philadelphia - Period: War - Enlisted by whom: William Bezeau - Listed on the Descriptive Roll of Colored Men, 1 Apr 1815.

Gilbert, Nathan - Private - 31st US Infantry - Company: Ethan Burnap - Age: 18 - Height: 5' 11 1/2" - Eyes: Black - Hair: Black - Complexion: Black - Born: Boston - Trade: Laborer - Enlistment date: 3 Apr 1814 - Place: Thetford, VT - Period: War - Enlisted by whom: Amos Brown - Discharged at Plattsburg, NY, on 4 Jun 1815.

Goforth, Daniel - Recruit - 26th US Infantry - Recruiting Detachment: William Bezeau - Age: 28 - Height: 5' 8" - Eyes: Black - Hair: Curly - Complexion: Chestnut - Born: Pennsylvania - Trade: Laborer - Enlistment date: 1 Jan 1815 - Place: Philadelphia - Period: 5 Yrs - Enlisted by whom: William Bezeau - Listed as a "Negro" in his service record; listed on the Descriptive Rolls of Colored Men, dated 25 Mar and 1 Apr 1815; discharged at Philadelphia on 1 May 1815.

Gormans, James (Gomaus) - Private - 11th US Infantry - Company: Samuel Holley - Age: 27 - Height: 5' 6" - Eyes: Black - Hair: Black - Complexion: Black - Trade: Baker - Enlistment date: 18 Jun 1812 - Period: 5 Yrs - Died on 19 Feb 1813.

Gossand, Abraham - Private - 26th US Infantry - Company: Wiliam Bezeau - Age: 25 - Height: 5' 6" - Eyes: Black - Hair: Curly - Complexion: Black - Born: New York - Trade: Seaman - Enlistment date: 22 Jan 1815 - Place: Philadelphia - Period: War - Enlisted by whom: William Bezeau - Listed on the Descriptive Roll of Colored Men, 1 Apr 1815.

Grashier, Francis - Private - 17th US Infantry - Company: William Adair - Other regiment: 3rd US Infantry - Age: 25 - Height: 5' 8" - Eyes: Black or Dark - Hair: Black or Dark - Complexion: Very Dark - Born: South America - Trade: Laborer - Enlistment date: 27 Apr 1814 - Place: Louisville, KY - Period: 5 Yrs - Enlisted by whom: Charles Querey - Discharged on 1 Feb 1816, Surgeon's Certificate of Disability for fractured shoulder.

Gray, John - Recruit - 26th US Infantry - Recruiting Detachment: William Bezeau - Age: 27 - Height: 5' 7" - Eyes: Black - Hair: Black - Complexion: Brown - Born: Delaware - Trade: Laborer - Enlistment date: 6 Nov 1814 - Place: Philadelphia - Period: War - Enlisted by whom: William Bezeau - Listed as "Col'd" in his service record; discharged on 30 Mar 1815 because of a disability.

Green, Robert - Private - US Light Artillery - Company: George Morris - Age: 44 - Height: 5' 4 1/2" - Eyes: Dark - Hair: Dark - Complexion: Dark - Born: Richmond, VA - Trade: Laborer - Enlistment date: 29 Sep 1814 - Place: Boston - Period: War - Discharged on 31 Mar 1815.

Grinton, Martin - Private - 10th US Infantry - Company: Robert Mitchell - Age: 20 - Height: 5' 9" - Eyes: Black - Hair: Black - Complexion: Black - Born: Wilkes County, NC - Trade: Farmer - Enlistment date: 23 Apr 1813 - Place: Wilkes County, NC - Period: 5 Yrs - Enlisted by whom: Willie Gordon - Pension: SO-27621 Rejected; served in Captains Robert Mitchell's, Emanuel Leigh's and Hippolite Villard's Companies, 10th Infantry - Listed as "Colored" in his service record; discharged at Elkton, MD, on 27 Aug 1815.

Grinton, Philip - Private - 10th US Infantry - Company: William Bailey - Other regiment: 8th US Infantry - Age: 20 - Height: 5' 8 1/2" - Eyes: Grey - Hair: Dark - Complexion: Dark - Born: Wilkes County, NC - Trade: Farmer - Enlistment date: 12 Aug 1813 - Place: Buncombe County, NC - Period: 5 Yrs - Enlisted by whom: Willie Gordon - Pension: Land bounty to Martin Grinton, brother & other heirs at law of Philip Grinton - BLW 25722-160-12 - Died at Portage de Sioux, MO, on 26 Sep 1815 from ague & fever.

Grinton, Robert - Private - 10th US Infantry - Company: Robert Mitchell - Age: 24 - Height: 5' 3" - Eyes: Black or dark - Hair: Black or Dark - Complexion: Dark or Yellow - Born: Wilksborough, NC - Trade: Farmer - Enlistment date: 23 Apr 1813 - Place: Wilkes County, NC - Period: 5 Yrs - Enlisted by whom: Willie Gordon - Listed as "Colored" in his service record; discharged on 26 Aug 1815, unfit for duty.

Hagar, Francis - Private - 9th US Infantry - Company: William Foster - Age: 40 - Height: 5' 9" - Eyes: Black or Light - Hair: Black - Complexion: Black - Born: Watertown, MA - Trade: Farmer - Enlistment date: 28 Jan 1813 - Place: Watertown, MA - Period: 5 Yrs - Enlisted by whom: Ebenezer Thompson - Pension: Old War IF-19968 - BLW 2980-160-12 - Discharged at Sackets Harbor, NY, on 3 Jul 1815 because of severe wounds.

Hagins, Jonathan (Hagans) - Private - 10th US Infantry - Company: Robert Mitchell - Other regiment: 8th

US Infantry - Age: 22 - Height: 5' 9" - Eyes: Dark - Hair: Black - Complexion: Yellow - Born: Sampson County, NC - Trade: Farmer - Enlistment date: 14 Jul 1813 - Place: Charlotte, NC - Period: 5 Yrs - Enlisted by whom: Alexander Brandon - Discharged at Fort Crawford, IL, on 23 May 1818.

Hall, Frederick – see William Williams

Halliard, Cyrus - Recruit - 26th US Infantry - Recruiting Detachment: William Bezeau - Age: 30 - Height: 5' 8" - Eyes: Black - Hair: Curly - Complexion: Black - Born: Pennsylvania - Trade: Farmer - Enlistment date: 23 Jan 1815 - Place: Philadelphia - Period: War - Enlisted by whom: William Bezeau - Listed on the Descriptive Roll of Colored Men, 1 Apr 1815.

Hames, John - Private - 30th US Infantry - Company: Gideon Spencer - Enlistment date: 8 Apr 1814 - Period: War - Colored soldier; discharged on 3 Jun 1814 for sore legs.

Haner, Peter - Recruit - 26th US Infantry - Recruiting Detachment: William Bezeau - Age: 20 - Height: 5' 3" - Eyes: Black - Hair: Curly - Complexion: Black - Born: New Jersey - Trade: Farmer - Enlistment date: 26 Jan 1815 - Place: Philadelphia - Period: War - Enlisted by whom: William Bezeau - Listed on the Descriptive Roll of Colored Men, 1 Apr 1815.

Harn, James - Recruit - 26th US Infantry - Recruiting Detachment: William Bezeau - Age: 27 - Height: 6' - Eyes: Black - Hair: Black - Complexion: Brown - Born: Virginia - Trade: Laborer - Enlistment date: 22 Oct 1814 - Place: Philadelphia - Period: War - Enlisted by whom: William Bezeau - BLW 7193-160-12 - Listed as "Col'd" in his service record; discharged at Philadelphia on 23 Mar 1815.

Harriot, Titus - Recruit - 26th US Infantry - Recruiting Detachment: William Bezeau - Age: 25 - Height: 5' 11" - Eyes: Black - Hair: Curly - Complexion: Black - Born: Pennsylvania - Trade: Farmer - Enlistment date: 8 Feb 1815 - Place: Philadelphia - Period: War - Enlisted by whom: William Bezeau - Listed on the Descriptive Roll of Colored Men, 1 Apr 1815.

Harriot, William - Private - 26th US Infantry - Recruiting Detachment: William Bezeau - Age: 24 - Height: 5' 9 1/2" - Eyes: Black - Hair: Curly - Complexion: Brown - Born: Pennsylvania - Trade: Farmer - Enlistment date: 24 Jan 1815 - Place: Philadelphia - Period: War - Enlisted by whom: William Bezeau - Listed on the Descriptive Roll of Colored Men, 1 Apr 1815.

Harris, Samuel - Recruit - 26th US Infantry - Recruiting Detachment: William Bezeau - Age: 24 - Height: 5' 10 1/2" - Eyes: Black - Hair: Black - Complexion: Black - Born: New York - Trade: Farmer - Enlistment date: 10 Oct 1814 - Place: Philadelphia - Period: 5 Yrs - Enlisted by whom: William Bezeau - Listed as a "Negro" and as "Colored" in his service record; discharged at Philadelphia on 7 May 1815, Surgeon's Certificate for Disability, unfit for service.

Harris, William - Private - 32nd US Infantry - Age: 26 - Height: 5' 5 1/2" - Eyes: Negro - Hair: Negro - Complexion: Negro - Born: Long Island, NY - Trade: Laborer - Enlistment date: 3 Feb 1815 - Enlisted by whom: Claudius La Grand - Listed as a "Negro" in his service record; discharged at Elkton, MD, on 17 Aug 1815 because of severe syphilis.

Harvey, William - Private - US Light Artillery - Company: John Bell - Age: 40 - Height: 5' 11" - Eyes: Black - Hair: Black - Complexion: Black - Born: Oxford, NH - Trade: Farmer - Enlistment date: 15 Jul 1812 - Place: Burlington, VT - Period: War - Enlisted by whom: William Campbell - Pension: Old War 10209; private in Second Lieutenant Nathaniel Dana's Detachment, US Light Artillery - Discharged at Boston on 31 Mar 1815.

Haskell, James - Private - US Light Artillery - Company: Benjamin Branch - Age: 18 - Height: 5' 10" - Eyes: Black - Hair: Dark or Black - Complexion: Black or Dark - Born: Standish, MA - Trade: Farmer - Enlistment date: 23 Feb 1813 - Place: Fort Preble, ME - Period: War - Enlisted by whom: Thomas Pitts - Discharged at Plattsburg, NY, on 31 May 1815.

Hatford, Samuel - Laborer - Corps of Artificers - Company: Alexander Parris - Listed as "Black" in *A List of Pensioners of the War of 1812*.

Hawkins, George - Recruit - 26th US Infantry - Recruiting Detachment: William Bezeau - Age: 21 - Height: 5' 9" - Eyes: Black - Hair: Curly - Complexion: Yellow - Born: New Jersey - Trade: Laborer - Enlistment date: 13 Oct 1814 - Place: Philadelphia - Period: War - Enlisted by whom: William Bezeau - Deserted on 1 Nov 1814.

Hazard, Daniel - Recruit - 26th US Infantry - Recruiting Detachment: William Bezeau - Age: 27 - Height: 5' 9" - Eyes: Black - Hair: Curly - Complexion: Brown - Born: Pennsylvania - Trade: Farmer - Enlistment date: 5 Feb 1815 - Place: Philadelphia - Period: War - Enlisted by whom: William Bezeau - Listed on the Descriptive Roll of Colored Men, 1 Apr 1815.

Hill, Isaac - Recruit - 26th US Infantry - Recruiting Detachment: William Bezeau - Age: 25 - Height: 5' 7" - Eyes: Black - Hair: Black - Complexion: Chestnut - Born: Philadelphia - Trade: Laborer - Enlistment date: 7 Oct 1814 - Place: Philadelphia - Period: War - Enlisted by whom: William Bezeau - BLW 7192-160-12 - Listed as "Col'd" in his service record; discharged at Philadelphia on 23 Mar 1815.

Hill, Levin - Recruit - 26th US Infantry - Recruiting Detachment: William Bezeau - Age: 22 - Height: 5' 7 1/2" - Eyes: Black - Hair: Curly - Complexion: Black - Born: Pennsylvania - Trade: Laborer - Enlistment date: 10 Oct 1814 - Place: Philadelphia - Period: 5 Yrs - Enlisted by whom: William Bezeau - Listed as "Col'd" in his service record; deserted on 20 Oct 1814 and again on 12 Jan 1815.

Hines, William - Private - 38th US Infantry - Company: James Smith - Age: 21 - Height: 5' 7" - Eyes: Brown - Hair: Dark - Complexion: Black - Born: Harford County, MD - Trade: Seaman - Enlistment date: 20 Feb 1814 - Place: Craney Island, VA - Period: War - Enlisted by whom: James Haslett - BLW 6565-160-12 - Discharged at Craney Island, VA, on 15 Mar 1815.

Hoggard, James (Hogart, Hoggart) - Private - 10th US Infantry - Company: George Vashan - Age: 20 - Height: 5' 6" - Eyes: Black - Hair: Black - Complexion: Yellow - Born: Bertie County, NC - Trade: Farmer - Enlistment date: 3 Jul 1812 - Period: 5 Yrs - Enlisted by whom: Richard Plummer - Discharged at Camp Experiment, AL, on 3 Aug 1817.

Holfer, Michael - Recruit - 26th US Infantry - Recruiting Detachment: William Bezeau - Age: 19 - Height: 5' 6" - Eyes: Blue - Hair: Curly - Complexion: Black - Born: Pennsylvania - Trade: Shoemaker - Enlistment date: 24 Jan 1815 - Place: Philadelphia - Period: War - Enlisted by whom: William Bezeau - Listed on the Descriptive Roll of Colored Men, 1 Apr 1815.

Horsey, James - Recruit - 26th US Infantry - Recruiting Detachment: William Bezeau - Age: 28 - Height: 5' 9" - Eyes: Black - Hair: Black - Complexion: Black - Born: New Jersey - Trade: Laborer - Enlistment date: 17 Oct 1814 - Place: Philadelphia - Period: War - Enlisted by whom: William Bezeau - Listed as "Col'd" in his service record.

Howard, Perry - Recruit Corporal - 26th US Infantry - Recruiting Detachment: William Bezeau -

Enlistment date: 27 Sep 1814 - Period: War - Enlisted by whom: James Whelpley - Listed as "Col'd" in his service record.

Howell, Jeffry - Recruit - 26th US Infantry - Recruiting Detachment: William Bezeau - Age: 24 - Height: 5' 7" - Eyes: Black - Hair: Curly - Complexion: Black - Born: Philadelphia - Trade: Laborer - Enlistment date: 14 Oct 1814 - Place: Philadelphia - Period: War - Enlisted by whom: William Bezeau - Listed as "Colored" in his service record; deserted on 18 Oct 1814.

Hubbert, Jeremiah (Hubbard) - Recruit - 26th US Infantry - Recruiting Detachment: William Bezeau - Age: 25 - Height: 5' 8" - Eyes: Black - Hair: Curly or Black - Complexion: Brown or Black - Born: Delaware - Enlistment date: 5 Jan 1815 - Place: Philadelphia - Period: War - Enlisted by whom: William Bezeau - Listed as a "Negro" in his service record; discharged at Philadelphia on 20 May 1815.

Huggs, Phil - Recruit - 26th US Infantry - Recruiting Detachment: William Bezeau - Age: 25 - Height: 5' 6" - Eyes: Black - Hair: Black - Complexion: Black - Born: New Jersey - Trade: Farmer - Enlistment date: 14 Oct 1814 - Place: Philadelphia - Period: War - Enlisted by whom: William Bezeau - Listed as "Col'd" in his service record; discharged at Philadelphia on 23 Mar 1815.

Hullings, Isaac (Hulling) - Recruit - 26th US Infantry - Recruiting Detachment: William Bezeau - Age: 29 - Height: 6' - Eyes: Black - Hair: Curly - Complexion: Black - Born: Pennsylvania - Trade: Farmer - Enlistment date: 16 Jan 1815 - Place: Philadelphia - Period: War - Enlisted by whom: William Bezeau - Listed on the Descriptive Roll of Colored Men, 1 Apr 1815; deserted on 27 Jan 1815.

Hunter, William - Recruit - 26th US Infantry - Recruiting Detachment: William Bezeau - Age: 34 - Height: 6' - Eyes: Black - Hair: Curly - Complexion: Black - Born: Delaware - Trade: Seaman - Enlistment date: 12 Feb 1815 - Place: Philadelphia - Period: War - Enlisted by whom: William Bezeau - Listed on the Descriptive Roll of Colored Men, 1 Apr 1815.

Hupler, Daniel - Recruit - 26th US Infantry - Recruiting Detachment: William Bezeau - Age: 27 - Height: 6' - Eyes: Black - Hair: Curly - Complexion: Black - Born: Pennsylvania - Trade: Farmer - Enlistment date: 9 Jun 1815 - Place: Philadelphia - Period: War - Enlisted by whom: William Bezeau - Listed on the Descriptive Roll of Colored Men, 1 Apr 1815; deserted on 18 Jan 1815.

Icard, Charles - Private - 44th US Infantry - Company: Anatole Peychaud - Age: 32 - Height: 5' 6 1/2" - Born: St. Nicholas Mole, San Domingo (Haiti) - Enlistment date: 17 Oct 1813 - Place: Powder Magazine, LA - Died on 17 May 1814.

Jack, Black - Servant - 27th US Infantry - Company: Christian Hartell - Probably Black due to his name "Black Jack" and for being a servant.

Jackson, Gabriel - Private - US Light Artillery - Company: John Bell - Age: 22 - Height: 5' 5 1/2" - Eyes: Black - Hair: Black - Complexion: Black - Born: Wilmington, DE - Trade: Mariner - Enlistment date: 10 Oct 1814 - Place: Boston - Period: War - Enlisted by whom: William Campbell - BLW 6808-160-12 - Discharged at Boston on 31 Mar 1815.

Jackson, George - Recruit - 26th US Infantry - Recruiting Detachment: William Bezeau - Age: 30 - Height: 5' 5" - Eyes: Black - Hair: Curly - Complexion: Black - Born: Maryland - Trade: Farmer - Enlistment date: 25 Dec 1814 - Place: Philadelphia - Period: 5 Yrs - Enlisted by whom: William Bezeau - Listed as "Col'd" in his service record.

Jackson, George - Private - US Light Artillery - Company: John McIntosh - Age: 24 - Height: 5' 7 3/4" - Eyes: Black - Hair: Black - Complexion: Black - Born: New York, NY - Trade: Mariner - Enlistment date: 13 Jul 1814 - Place: Boston - Period: War - Enlisted by whom: Samuel Washburn - Discharged at Plattsburg, NY, on 31 May 1815.

Jackson, James Z. - Recruit - 26th US Infantry - Recruiting Detachment: William Bezeau - Age: 22 - Height: 5' 6" - Eyes: Black - Hair: Curly - Complexion: Black - Born: Delaware - Trade: Sailor - Enlistment date: 12 Feb 1815 - Place: Philadelphia - Period: War - Enlisted by whom: William Bezeau - BLW 1042-320-12 - Listed on the Descriptive Roll of Colored Men, 1 Apr 1815; discharged at Philadelphia on 20 Mar 1815.

Jackson, John - Private - US Light Artillery - Company: John McIntosh - Age: 21 - Height: 5' 6" - Eyes: Black - Hair: Black - Complexion: Black - Born: New Orleans - Trade: Mariner - Enlistment date: 15 Jul 1814 - Place: Boston - Period: War - Enlisted by whom: Samuel Washburn - Discharged at Plattsburg, NY, on 31 May 1815.

Jackson, John - Recruit - 26th US Infantry - Recruiting Detachment: William Bezeau - Age: 22 - Height: 5' 6" - Eyes: Black - Hair: Curly - Complexion: Brown - Born: Pennsylvania - Trade: Laborer - Enlistment date: 26 Dec 1814 - Place: Philadelphia - Period: War - Enlisted by whom: William Bezeau - BLW 536-320-12 - Discharged at Philadelphia on 20 Mar 1815.

Jackson Jr., John - Recruit - 26th US Infantry - Recruiting Detachment: William Bezeau - Age: 25 - Height: 5' 11" - Eyes: Black - Hair: Curly - Complexion: Black - Born: Connecticut - Trade: Farmer - Enlistment date: 15 Nov 1814 - Place: Philadelphia - Period: War - Enlisted by whom: William Bezeau - Listed as "Col'd" in his service record; deserted on 5 Dec 1814.

Jackson, William - Recruit - 26th US Infantry - Recruiting Detachment: William Bezeau - Age: 25 - Height: 5' 5" - Eyes: Black - Hair: Curly - Complexion: Black - Born: Georgia - Enlistment date: 24 Jan 1815 - Place: Philadelphia - Period: War - Enlisted by whom: William Bezeau - Listed on the Descriptive Roll of Colored Men, 1 Apr 1815.

James, David - Recruit - 26th US Infantry - Recruiting Detachment: William Bezeau - Age: 21 - Height: 5' 9" - Eyes: Grey - Hair: Curly - Complexion: Yellow - Born: Pennsylvania - Trade: Laborer - Enlistment date: 12 Feb 1815 - Place: Philadelphia - Period: 5 Yrs - Enlisted by whom: William Bezeau - Pension: Land bounty to Sarah James, sister & only heir at law of David James, deceased; land bounty annulled, not entitled to land - BLW 19232-160-12 Cancelled - Listed on the Descriptive Roll of Colored Men, 1 Apr 1815; died on 2 Mar 1815.

James, George - Recruit - 26th US Infantry - Recruiting Detachment: William Bezeau - Age: 21 - Height: 5' 8 1/2" - Eyes: Black - Hair: Black - Complexion: Sallow - Born: Pennsylvania - Trade: Farmer - Enlistment date: 13 Sep 1814 - Place: Philadelphia - Period: War - Enlisted by whom: William Bezeau - Listed as "Col'd" in his service record; deserted on 25 Sep 1814.

James, James Frederick - Private - 10th US Infantry - Age: 20 - Height: 5' 3 5/8" - Eyes: Man of color - Hair: Man of color - Complexion: Man of color - Born: Bertie County, NC - Trade: Wheelwright - Enlistment date: 17 Aug 1812 - Period: 5 Yrs - Listed as a "Man of Color" in his service record.

Jamison, Edward - Recruit - 26th US Infantry - Recruiting Detachment: William Bezeau - Age: 22 - Height: 5' 4" - Eyes: Black - Hair: Curly - Complexion: Yellow - Born: Pennsylvania - Trade: Seaman - Enlistment date: 9 Feb 1815 - Place: Philadelphia - Period: War - Enlisted by whom: William Bezeau - Pension: Land bounty to Abraham Jamison, cousin & only heir at law of Edward

Jamison, deceased; died before 21 Oct 1819; first bounty was cancelled because Jamison was entitled to 320 acres of land - BLW 833-320-14 Cancelled; BLW 1040-320-14 - Listed on the Descriptive Roll of Colored Men, 1 Apr 1815; discharged under the general order of 4 Mar 1815.

Jasper, Peter - Recruit - 26th US Infantry - Recruiting Detachment: William Bezeau - Age: 18 - Height: 5' 5" - Eyes: Black - Hair: Curly - Complexion: Black - Born: Maryland - Trade: Laborer - Enlistment date: 21 Jan 1815 - Place: Philadelphia - Period: War - Enlisted by whom: William Bezeau - Listed on the Descriptive Roll of Colored Men, 1 Apr 1815; deserted on 27 Jan 1815.

Jefferson, Isaac - Recruit - 26th US Infantry - Recruiting Detachment: William Bezeau - Age: 28 - Height: 5' 6" - Eyes: Black - Hair: Curly - Complexion: Black - Born: Pennsylvania - Trade: Blacksmith - Enlistment date: 4 Dec 1814 - Place: Philadelphia - Period: War - Enlisted by whom: William Bezeau - Listed as "Col'd" in his service record; discharged at Philadelphia on 1 May 1815.

Jister, Alexander - Recruit - 26th US Infantry - Recruiting Detachment: William Bezeau - Age: 28 - Height: 5' 4" - Eyes: Black - Hair: Curly - Complexion: Black - Born: Pennsylvania - Trade: Farmer - Enlistment date: 18 Jan 1815 - Place: Philadelphia - Period: War - Enlisted by whom: William Bezeau - Listed on the Descriptive Roll of Colored Men, 1 Apr 1815.

Johnson, Alexander J. - Recruit - 26th US Infantry - Recruiting Detachment: William Bezeau - Age: 31 - Height: 5' 4" - Eyes: Black - Hair: Curly - Complexion: not stated - Born: Africa - Trade: Waiter - Enlistment date: 7 Dec 1814 - Place: Philadelphia - Period: War - Enlisted by whom: William Bezeau - BLW 5288-160-12 - Listed as "Colored" in his service record; discharged at Philadelphia on 20 Mar 1815.

Johnson, Amos - Private - 24th US Infantry - Company: Silas Stephens - Age: 33 - Height: 5' 7" - Eyes: Black or Dark - Hair: Dark - Complexion: Black or Dark - Born: Mecklenburg County, VA - Trade: Farmer - Enlistment date: 9 Dec 1814 - Period: 5 Yrs - Enlisted by whom: William Chilton - Listed as "Black" in his service record.

Johnson, Isaac - Recruit - 26th US Infantry - Recruiting Detachment: William Bezeau - Age: 40 - Height: 5' 11" - Eyes: Hazel - Hair: Curly - Complexion: Yellow - Born: Delaware - Trade: Miller - Enlistment date: 25 Oct 1814 - Place: Philadelphia - Period: 5 Yrs - Enlisted by whom: William Bezeau - Listed as "Col'd" in his service record.

Johnson, Jacob - Recruit - 26th US Infantry - Recruiting Detachment: William Bezeau - Age: 22 - Height: 5' 6" - Eyes: Black - Hair: Curly - Complexion: Black - Born: Pennsylvania - Trade: Farmer - Enlistment date: 21 Oct 1814 - Place: Philadelphia - Period: 5 Yrs - Enlisted by whom: William Bezeau - Listed as "Col'd" in his service record; discharged on 20 May 1815.

Johnson, James - Recruit - 26th US Infantry - Recruiting Detachment: William Bezeau - Age: 35 - Height: 5' 9" - Eyes: Black - Hair: Curly - Complexion: Yellow - Born: Maryland - Trade: Laborer - Enlistment date: 24 Nov 1814 - Place: Philadelphia - Period: War - Enlisted by whom: William Bezeau - BLW 10293-160-12 - Listed as "Col'd" in his service record; discharged at Philadelphia on 20 Mar 1815.

Johnson, James - Private - 14th US Infantry - Company: David Cummings - Age: 19 - Height: 5' 5" - Eyes: Dark - Hair: Brown - Complexion: Yellow - Born: Baltimore - Trade: Shoemaker - Enlistment date: 6 Nov 1814 - Place: Camp Snowden, MD - Period: 5 Yrs - Enlisted by whom: James Riddle.

Johnson, James F. - Recruit - 26th US Infantry - Recruiting Detachment: William Bezeau - Age: 21 - Height: 5' 10" - Eyes: Black - Hair: Curly - Complexion: Brown - Born: Delaware - Trade: Sailor - Enlistment date: 12 Jan 1815 - Place: Philadelphia - Period: War - Enlisted by whom: William Bezeau - BLW 10294-160-12 - Listed on the Descriptive Roll of Colored Men, 1 Apr 1815; discharged at Philadelphia on 20 May 1815.

Johnson, John - Private - US Light Artillery - Company: George Morris - Age: 22 - Height: 5' 7 1/2" - Eyes: Black - Hair: Black - Complexion: Black - Born: Danbury, CT - Trade: Laborer - Enlistment date: 22 Sep 1814 - Place: Dedham, MA - Period: War - Enlisted by whom: William Campbell - Discharged on 31 Mar 1815 on account of being a Negro and unfit to accompany American soldiers.

Johnson, Joseph T. - Recruit - 26th US Infantry - Recruiting Detachment: William Bezeau - Age: 20 - Height: 5' 3" - Eyes: Black - Hair: Curly - Complexion: Black - Born: Trinidad, West Indies - Trade: Seaman - Enlistment date: 3 Feb 1815 - Place: Philadelphia - Period: War - Enlisted by whom: William Bezeau - BLW 311-320-14 - Listed on the Descriptive Roll of Colored Men, 1 Apr 1815; discharged at Philadelphia on 20 Mar 1815.

Johnson, Richard - Private - US Light Artillery - Company: George Morris - Age: 25 - Height: 5' 5" - Eyes: Dark - Hair: Black - Complexion: Black - Born: Danbury, CT - Trade: Laborer - Enlistment date: 22 Sep 1814 - Place: Dedham, MA - Period: 5 Yrs - Enlisted by whom: William Campbell - Discharged on 31 Mar 1815 on account of being a Negro and not fit to accompany American soldiers.

Johnson, Samuel - Private - US Light Artillery - Company: John Bell - Age: 30 - Height: 5' 8" - Eyes: Black - Hair: Black - Complexion: Black - Born: Long Island, NY - Trade: Mariner - Enlistment date: 29 Aug 1814 - Place: Boston - Period: War - Enlisted by whom: Samuel Washburn - Discharged on 31 Mar 1815.

Johnson, Thomas - Recruit - 26th US Infantry - Recruiting Detachment: William Bezeau - Age: 29 - Height: 5' 7" - Eyes: Black - Hair: Curly - Complexion: Brown - Born: Washington, DC - Trade: Laborer - Enlistment date: 13 Nov 1814 - Place: Philadelphia - Period: War - Enlisted by whom: William Bezeau - BLW 7195-160-12 - Listed as "Col'd" in his service record; discharged at Philadelphia on 25 Mar 1815.

Johnson, William - Private - 9th US Infantry - Company: Otis Fisher - Age: 23 - Height: 5' 3 1/2" - Eyes: Black - Hair: Black - Complexion: Black - Born: Quebeck, MA - Trade: Farmer - Enlistment date: 7 Dec 1814 - Place: Pittsfield, MA - Period: War - Enlisted by whom: Benoni Allen - BLW 12745-160-12 - Discharged at Pittsfield, MA, on 31 Mar 1815.

Johnson, William - Recruit - 26th US Infantry - Recruiting Detachment: William Bezeau - Age: 28 - Height: 5' 4" - Eyes: Black - Hair: Black - Complexion: Black - Born: Rhode Island - Trade: Sail maker - Enlistment date: 3 Nov 1814 - Place: Philadelphia - Period: 5 Yrs - Enlisted by whom: William Bezeau - Listed as "Colored" in his service record; discharged on 1 May 1815, not fit for military duty (medical reason).

Jones, Henry - Recruit - 26th US Infantry - Recruiting Detachment: William Bezeau - Age: 20 - Height: 5' 6" - Eyes: Dark - Hair: Curly - Complexion: Black - Born: Delaware - Trade: Laborer - Enlistment date: 4 Dec 1814 - Place: Philadelphia - Period: War - Enlisted by whom: William Bezeau - Listed as "Col'd" in his service record; died in general hospital on 9 Jan 1815.

Jones, Ira - Private - 30th US Infantry - Company: Sylvanus Danforth - Other regiment: US Light Artillery - Age: 19 - Height: 5' 4" - Eyes: Black - Hair: Curly - Complexion: Black - Born: Worthington, MA - Trade: Farmer - Enlistment date: 18 Dec 1814 - Place: Ballston - Period: 5 Yrs - Enlisted by whom: Gideon Brownson - Listed as a "Negro" in his service record.

Jones, Isaac - Recruit - 26th US Infantry - Recruiting Detachment: William Bezeau - Age: 44 - Height: 5' 9 1/2" - Eyes: Brown - Hair: Dark - Complexion: Dark - Born: Pennsylvania - Trade: Laborer - Enlistment date: 2 Dec 1814 - Place: Philadelphia - Period: 5 Yrs - Enlisted by whom: William Bezeau - Listed as "Col'd" in his service record; discharged at Philadelphia on 20 May 1815.

Jones, Rowland - Fifer - 10th US Infantry - Company: Robert Mitchell - Other regiment: 8th US Infantry - Age: 28 - Height: 5' 9" - Eyes: Black - Hair: Black - Complexion: Yellow - Born: Lunenburg, VA - Trade: Ditcher - Enlistment date: 19 Jun 1812 - Place: Person, NC - Period: 5 Yrs - Enlisted by whom: Robert Mitchell - BLW 26801-160-12 - Discharged at Pass Christian, MS, on 19 Jun 1817.

Jones, Solomon - Recruit - 26th US Infantry - Recruiting Detachment: William Bezeau - Age: 40 - Height: 5' 8" - Eyes: Grey - Hair: Brown - Complexion: Dark - Born: Pennsylvania - Trade: Laborer - Enlistment date: 30 Aug 1814 - Place: Philadelphia - Period: 5 Yrs - Enlisted by whom: William Bezeau - Listed as "Col'd" in his service record; discharged at Philadelphia on 1 Jun 1815.

Joseph, Daniel - Recruit - 26th US Infantry - Recruiting Detachment: William Bezeau - Age: 24 - Height: 5' 8" - Eyes: Black - Hair: Curly - Complexion: Black - Born: Delaware - Trade: Farmer - Enlistment date: 7 Feb 1815 - Place: Philadelphia - Period: War - Enlisted by whom: William Bezeau - Listed on the Descriptive Roll of Colored Men, 1 Apr 1815.

Joseph, John - Recruit - 26th US Infantry - Recruiting Detachment: William Bezeau - Age: 23 - Height: 5' 5" - Eyes: Black - Hair: Curly - Complexion: Yellow - Born: Lisbon, Portugal - Trade: Mariner - Enlistment date: 25 Dec 1814 - Place: Philadelphia - Period: 5 Yrs - Enlisted by whom: William Bezeau - Listed as "Col'd" and as a "Black man" in his service record; discharged at Philadelphia on 20 May 1815.

Junior, Ceazer - Recruit - 26th US Infantry - Recruiting Detachment: William Bezeau - Age: 40 - Height: 5' 3" - Eyes: Black - Hair: Curly - Complexion: Black - Born: Pennsylvania - Trade: Laborer - Enlistment date: 29 Nov 1814 - Place: Philadelphia - Period: 5 Yrs - Enlisted by whom: William Bezeau - Listed as "Col'd" in his service record; discharged on 20 May 1815.

Karmon, Peter (Kannon) - Recruit - 26th US Infantry - Recruiting Detachment: William Bezeau - Age: 17 - Height: 5' 4" - Eyes: Black - Hair: Curly - Complexion: Brown - Born: Maryland - Trade: Farmer - Enlistment date: 16 Jan 1815 - Place: Philadelphia - Period: War - Enlisted by whom: William Bezeau - Listed on the Descriptive Roll of Colored Men, 1 Apr 1815.

Kellehorn, James (Kelliharn) - Private - US Light Artillery - Company: John McIntosh - Age: 21 - Height: 5' 6" - Eyes: Black - Hair: Black - Complexion: Black - Born: Boston - Trade: Rope maker - Enlistment date: 19 Jul 1814 - Place: Boston - Period: War - Enlisted by whom: Samuel Washburn - Discharged at Plattsburg, NY, on 31 May 1815.

Kelley, Ezekiel - Recruit - 26th US Infantry - Recruiting Detachment: William Bezeau - Age: 19 - Height: 5' 6" - Eyes: Black - Hair: Curly - Complexion: Black - Born: Jamaica, West Indies - Trade: Seaman - Enlistment date: 19 Jan 1815 - Place: Philadelphia - Period: War - Enlisted by whom: William Bezeau - Listed on the Descriptive Roll of Colored Men, 1 Apr 1815.

Kimbert, Moses - Recruit - 26th US Infantry - Recruiting Detachment: William Bezeau - Age: 21 - Height: 5' 8" - Eyes: Black - Hair: Curly - Complexion: Black - Born: New York - Trade: Farmer - Enlistment date: 2 Feb 1815 - Place: Philadelphia - Period: War - Enlisted by whom: William Bezeau - Listed on the Descriptive Roll of Colored Men, 1 Apr 1815.

Kingsley, Samuel - Recruit Sergeant - 26th US Infantry - Recruiting Detachment: William Bezeau - Age: 21 - Height: 5' 6" - Born: Havre de Grace, MD - Enlistment date: 8 Sep 1814 - Place: Baltimore - Period: War - Enlisted by whom: James Whelpley - Listed as "Col'd" in his service record.

Kirkpatrick, Ezekiel - Private - 39th US Infantry - Company: George Hallum - Enlistment date: 15 Jan 1815 - Reported as a Negro; discharged on 14 Jan 1815.

Kisling, James - Recruit - 26th US Infantry - Recruiting Detachment: William Bezeau - Age: 27 - Height: 5' 6" - Eyes: Black - Hair: Curly - Complexion: Brown - Born: Maryland - Trade: Farmer - Enlistment date: 19 Jan 1815 - Place: Philadelphia - Period: War - Enlisted by whom: William Bezeau - Listed on the Descriptive Roll of Colored Men, 1 Apr 1815.

Knight, John - Recruit - 26th US Infantry - Recruiting Detachment: William Bezeau - Age: 21 - Height: 5' 6 1/2" - Eyes: Black - Hair: Curly - Complexion: Yellow - Born: Pennsylvania - Trade: Laborer - Enlistment date: 24 Nov 1814 - Place: Philadelphia - Period: War - Enlisted by whom: William Bezeau - Listed as "Col'd" in his service record.

La Cruse – see Francis L. Cruse

Ladine, Noah - Recruit - 26th US Infantry - Recruiting Detachment: William Bezeau - Age: 28 - Height: 5' 8" - Eyes: Black - Hair: Black - Complexion: Black - Born: Delaware - Trade: Miller - Enlistment date: 7 Oct 1814 - Place: Philadelphia - Period: 5 Yrs - Enlisted by whom: William Bezeau - Listed as "Colored" in his service record; discharged at Philadelphia on 24 May 1815; he has two service records recorded. The second service record is listed under Noah Lowdine, and it indicates that he is a "Blackman."

Ladman, Charles - Recruit - 26th US Infantry - Recruiting Detachment: William Bezeau - Age: 31 - Height: 5' 8" - Eyes: Black - Hair: Curly - Complexion: Brown - Born: Pennsylvania - Trade: Farmer - Enlistment date: 13 Jan 1815 - Place: Philadelphia - Period: War - Enlisted by whom: William Bezeau - Not listed on the Descriptive Roll of Colored Men, 1 Apr 1815, but on the normal Descriptive Roll for 1 Apr 1815 (for Whites).

Lambert, George - Private - 26th US Infantry - Recruiting Detachment: William Bezeau - Enlistment date: 5 Jan 1815 - Period: War - Enlisted by whom: William Bezeau - Listed as a "Colored man."

Lambert, Samuel - Recruit - 26th US Infantry - Recruiting Detachment: William Bezeau - Age: 24 - Height: 5' 10" - Eyes: Black - Hair: Curly - Complexion: Brown - Born: Pennsylvania - Trade: Laborer - Enlistment date: 19 Jan 1815 - Place: Philadelphia - Period: War - Enlisted by whom: William Bezeau - Listed on the Descriptive Roll of Colored Men, 1 Apr 1815.

Lang, William - Recruit - 26th US Infantry - Recruiting Detachment: William Bezeau - Age: 22 - Height: 5' 6" - Eyes: Black - Hair: Curly - Complexion: Dark - Born: Pennsylvania - Trade: Farmer - Enlistment date: 11 Nov 1814 - Place: Philadelphia - Period: War - Enlisted by whom: William Bezeau - BLW 7195-160-12 - Listed as "Colored" in his service record; discharged at Philadelphia on 23 Mar 1815.

Larkin, Manuel A. - Private - 3rd US Infantry - Company: Robert Moore - Age: 29 - Height: 5' 6" - Eyes: Black - Hair: Black - Complexion: Black - Trade: Laborer - Enlistment date: 3 May 1814 - Place: Fort Claiborne, AL - Period: 5 Yrs - Enlisted by whom: Robert Moore - Deserted on 9 May 1815; also listed as Manuel or Manwell Alarkin.

Larkman, George - Recruit - 26th US Infantry - Recruiting Detachment: William Bezeau - Age: 21 - Height: 5' 5" - Eyes: Black - Hair: Curly - Complexion: Black - Born: Pennsylvania - Trade: Laborer - Enlistment date: 7 Jan 1815 - Place: Philadelphia - Period: War - Enlisted by whom: William Bezeau - Listed on the Descriptive Roll of Colored Men, 1 Apr 1815.

Lawrence, Nathaniel - Laborer - Corps of Artificers - Company: Alexander Parris - Listed as "Black" in *A List of Pensioners of the War of 1812*.

Lawrence, Peter - Private - US Light Artillery - Company: George Morris - Age: 23 - Height: 5' 8" - Eyes: Black - Hair: Black - Complexion: Black - Born: Petersburg, VA - Trade: Mariner - Enlistment date: 7 Oct 1814 - Place: Boston - Period: War - Enlisted by whom: William Campbell - BLW 13175-160-12 - Discharged at Boston on 31 Mar 1815.

Leadway – see Benjamin Lodway

Lee, Andrew - Private - US Light Artillery - Company: John Bell - Age: 21 - Height: 5' 7 1/2" - Eyes: Black - Hair: Black - Complexion: Black - Born: Northampton, MA - Trade: Farmer - Enlistment date: 23 Sep 1814 - Place: Boston - Period: War - Enlisted by whom: William Campbell - Discharged on 31 Mar 1815.

Lee, Jeremiah - Recruit - 26th US Infantry - Recruiting Detachment: William Bezeau - Age: 23 - Height: 5' 7" - Eyes: Black - Hair: Curly or Black - Complexion: Black - Born: Delaware - Trade: Laborer - Enlistment date: 1 Jan 1815 - Place: Philadelphia - Period: 5 Yrs - Enlisted by whom: William Bezeau - Listed as "Colored" and as a "Blackman" in his service record; discharged at Philadelphia on 20 May 1815.

Lee, Thomas - Recruit - 26th US Infantry - Recruiting Detachment: William Bezeau - Age: 19 - Height: 5' 6" - Eyes: Hazel - Hair: Curly - Complexion: Black - Born: New Jersey - Trade: Laborer - Enlistment date: 6 Jan 1815 - Place: Philadelphia - Period: War - Enlisted by whom: William Bezeau - BLW 741-320-12 - Listed on the Descriptive Roll of Colored Men, 1 Apr 1815; discharged on 20 Mar 1815.

Leubert, George - Recruit - 26th US Infantry - Recruiting Detachment: William Bezeau - Age: 31 - Height: 5' 5" - Eyes: Black - Hair: Curly - Complexion: Black - Born: Pennsylvania - Trade: Laborer - Enlistment date: 5 Jan 1815 - Place: Philadelphia - Period: War - Enlisted by whom: William Bezeau - Listed on the Descriptive Roll of Colored Men, 1 Apr 1815.

Lewis, Benjamin - Recruit - 26th US Infantry - Recruiting Detachment: William Bezeau - Age: 29 - Height: 5' 6" - Eyes: Black - Hair: Curly - Complexion: Brown - Born: Pennsylvania - Trade: Laborer - Enlistment date: 2 Nov 1814 - Place: Philadelphia - Period: War - Enlisted by whom: William Bezeau - Listed as "Col'd" in his service record.

Lewis, Joseph - Servant - 27th US Infantry - Company: Christian Hartell - Listed as a "Black boy."

Lewis, Prince - Recruit - 26th US Infantry - Recruiting Detachment: William Bezeau - Age: 23 - Height:

5' 8 1/2" - Eyes: Black - Hair: Curly - Complexion: Mulatto - Born: New Jersey - Trade: Farmer - Enlistment date: 30 Dec 1814 - Place: Philadelphia - Period: War - Enlisted by whom: William Bezeau - BLW 743-320-12 - Listed as "Col'd" in his service record; discharged on 31 Mar 1815.

Lewis, Robert - Private - US Light Artillery - Company: George Morris - Age: 22 - Height: 5' 2 7/8" - Eyes: Black - Hair: Black - Complexion: Black - Born: Chester, VA - Trade: Mariner - Enlistment date: 3 Aug 1814 - Place: Salem or Boston, MA - Period: War - Enlisted by whom: Samuel Washburn - Discharged at Boston on 31 Mar 1815.

Lillman, Joseph - Recruit - 26th US Infantry - Recruiting Detachment: William Bezeau - Enlistment date: 20 Sep 1814 - Place: Philadelphia - Period: War - Enlisted by whom: William Bezeau - Listed as "Col'd" in his service record.

Limmon, Charles - Recruit - 26th US Infantry - Recruiting Detachment: William Bezeau - Age: 25 - Height: 5' 7" - Eyes: Black - Hair: Curly - Complexion: Black - Born: Pennsylvania - Trade: Laborer - Enlistment date: 15 Jan 1815 - Place: Philadelphia - Period: War - Enlisted by whom: William Bezeau - Listed on the Descriptive Roll of Colored Men, 1 Apr 1815.

Linds, Samuel - Private - 11th US Infantry - Company: Benjamin Smead - Age: 20 - Height: 5' 10" - Eyes: Black - Hair: Black - Complexion: Black color - Trade: Husbandman - Enlistment date: 1 Mar 1813 - Period: 5 Yrs - Enlisted by whom: Benjamin Smead - Discharged at Fort Columbus, Governor's Island, NY, on 19 Sep 1815 for disability.

Liston, John - Recruit - 26th US Infantry - Recruiting Detachment: William Bezeau - Age: 24 - Height: 5' 5" - Eyes: Black - Hair: Curly - Complexion: Dark - Born: Philadelphia - Trade: Farmer - Enlistment date: 21 Nov 1814 - Place: Philadelphia - Period: 5 Yrs - Enlisted by whom: William Bezeau - Listed as "Col'd" in his service record; discharged at Philadelphia on 7 May 1815.

Little, Lymus W. - Private - US Light Artillery - Age: 35 - Height: 5' 4 1/2" - Eyes: Black - Hair: Black - Complexion: Black - Born: Slainfield, CT - Trade: Mariner - Enlistment date: 10 Oct 1814 - Place: Boston - Period: War - Enlisted by whom: William Campbell - Discharged on 31 Mar 1815.

Little, William Allen - Private - 26th US Infantry - Recruiting Detachment: William Bezeau - Age: 32 - Height: 5' 10 1/2" - Eyes: Dark - Hair: Brown - Complexion: Brown - Born: Philadelphia - Trade: Ship joiner - Enlistment date: 10 Sep 1814 - Place: Philadelphia - Period: War - Discharged at Lazaretto, PA, by Dr. Heilman.

Littleton, Samuel - Private - 31st US Infantry - Company: Rufus Stewart - Age: 39 - Height: 5' 7" - Eyes: Black - Hair: Black - Complexion: Black - Born: Charlestown, MA - Trade: Farmer - Enlistment date: 26 Apr 1814 - Place: Montpelier, VT - Period: War - Enlisted by whom: Harvey Gillman - Discharged at Plattsburg, NY, on 3 Jun 1815.

Lodway, Benjamin - Recruit - 26th US Infantry - Recruiting Detachment: William Bezeau - Age: 27 - Height: 5' 8" - Eyes: Black - Hair: Curly - Complexion: Black - Born: Pennsylvania - Trade: Laborer - Enlistment date: 23 Jan 1815 - Place: Philadelphia - Period: War - Enlisted by whom: William Bezeau - Listed on the Descriptive Roll of Colored Men, 1 Apr 1815.

Looks, Samuel - Musician - 2nd US Rifles - Company: Batteal Harrison - Age: 20 - Height: 5' 5" - Eyes: Black - Hair: Black - Complexion: Black - Born: Quebec, UC - Trade: Musician - Enlistment date: 4 Jul 1814 - Place: Chillicothe, OH - Period: 5 Yrs - Enlisted by whom: Batteal Harrison.

Lowdine – see Noah Ladine

Lower, Joseph - Recruit - 26th US Infantry - Recruiting Detachment: William Bezeau - Age: 28 - Height: 5' 6" - Eyes: Black - Hair: Curly - Complexion: Dark - Born: Pennsylvania - Trade: Laborer - Enlistment date: 6 Feb 1815 - Place: Philadelphia - Period: War - Enlisted by whom: William Bezeau - Listed as "Col'd" in his service record.

Loyd, Samuel - Recruit - 26th US Infantry - Recruiting Detachment: William Bezeau - Age: 36 - Height: 5' 9 1/2" - Eyes: Black - Hair: Curly - Complexion: Brown - Born: Pennsylvania - Trade: Farmer - Enlistment date: 14 Jan 1815 - Place: Philadelphia - Period: War - Enlisted by whom: William Bezeau - Listed on the Descriptive Roll of Colored Men, 1 Apr 1815.

Lubby, Thomas - Recruit - 26th US Infantry - Recruiting Detachment: William Bezeau - Age: 30 - Height: 5' 11" - Eyes: Black - Hair: Curly - Complexion: Black - Born: Delaware - Trade: Laborer - Enlistment date: 9 Feb 1815 - Place: Philadelphia - Period: War - Enlisted by whom: William Bezeau - Listed on the Descriptive Roll of Colored Men, 1 Apr 1815.

Luff, Henry - Recruit - 26th US Infantry - Recruiting Detachment: William Bezeau - Age: 27 - Height: 5' 9" - Eyes: Dark - Hair: Black - Complexion: Brown - Born: Pennsylvania - Trade: Sailor - Enlistment date: 27 May 1814 - Place: Philadelphia - Period: 5 Yrs - Enlisted by whom: William Bezeau - Listed as "Col'd" in his service record.

Luke, Seth - Recruit - 26th US Infantry - Recruiting Detachment: William Bezeau - Age: 26 - Height: 6' - Eyes: Black - Hair: Curly - Complexion: Black - Born: Pennsylvania - Trade: Laborer - Enlistment date: 27 Jan 1815 - Place: Philadelphia - Period: War - Enlisted by whom: William Bezeau - Listed on the Descriptive Roll of Colored Men, 1 Apr 1815.

Lynes, William - Private - 30th US Infantry - Company: Gideon Spencer - Age: 21 - Height: 5' 3" - Eyes: Black - Hair: Curly - Complexion: Black - Born: Wilmington, MA - Trade: Farmer - Enlistment date: 2 Apr 1814 - Place: Burlington, VT - Period: 5 Yrs - Enlisted by whom: William Barney - On duty with the US Navy after 6 Sep 1814 (probably Lake Champlain); deserted at Burlington, VT, on 30 Apr 1815.

Madber, Thomas - Recruit - 26th US Infantry - Recruiting Detachment: William Bezeau - Age: 24 - Height: 5' 11" - Eyes: Black - Hair: Curly - Complexion: Black - Born: Pennsylvania - Trade: Farmer - Enlistment date: 23 Jan 1815 - Place: Philadelphia - Period: War - Enlisted by whom: William Bezeau - Listed on the Descriptive Roll of Colored Men, 1 Apr 1815.

Maddy, Levin - Recruit - 26th US Infantry - Recruiting Detachment: William Bezeau - Age: 30 - Height: 5' 6" - Eyes: Black - Hair: Black - Complexion: Black - Born: Maryland - Trade: Laborer - Enlistment date: 9 Oct 1814 - Place: Philadelphia - Period: War - Enlisted by whom: William Bezeau - BLW 10295-160-12 - Listed as "Col'd" in his service record; discharged at Philadelphia on 20 Mar 1815.

Manner, James - Recruit - 26th US Infantry - Recruiting Detachment: William Bezeau - Age: 22 - Height: 5' 4" - Eyes: Black - Hair: Curly - Complexion: Black - Born: New Jersey - Trade: Farmer - Enlistment date: 8 Feb 1815 - Place: Philadelphia - Period: War - Enlisted by whom: William Bezeau - Listed on the Descriptive Roll of Colored Men, 1 Apr 1815.

Marcus, Richard - Recruit - 26th US Infantry - Recruiting Detachment: William Bezeau - Age: 20 - Height: 5' 6 1/2" - Eyes: Black - Hair: Curly - Complexion: Brown - Born: Pennsylvania - Trade:

Laborer - Enlistment date: 18 Dec 1814 - Place: Philadelphia - Period: War - Enlisted by whom: William Bezeau - Listed as "Col'd" in his service record.

Marshall, Samuel W. - Laborer - Corps of Artificers - Company: Alexander Parris - Listed as "Black" in *A List of Pensioners of the War of 1812*.

Martin, John - Private - 14th US Infantry - Company: David Cummings - Age: 16 - Height: 4' 4" - Born: Port Tobacco, MD - Trade: Soldier - Enlistment date: 22 Oct 1814 - Place: Alexandria, DC - Period: War - BLW 21317-160-12 - Discharged at Baltimore on 16 Mar 1815.

Masters, William - Private - US Light Artillery - Company: George Melven - Age: 17 - Height: 5' 3 1/2" - Eyes: Black - Hair: Black - Complexion: Black - Born: Andover, NH - Trade: Blacksmith - Enlistment date: 5 Feb 1813 - Place: NH, Windsor - Period: 5 Yrs - Enlisted by whom: James Cobb - Discharged on 28 Aug 1815 by civil authority.

Mathias, Charles (Mathews) - Recruit - 26th US Infantry - Recruiting Detachment: William Bezeau - Age: 26 - Height: 5' - Eyes: Brown - Hair: Black - Complexion: Chestnut - Born: Maryland - Trade: Shoemaker - Enlistment date: 8 Oct 1814 - Place: Philadelphia - Period: 5 Yrs - Enlisted by whom: William Bezeau - Listed as "Colored" in his service record; discharged at Philadelphia on 16 May 1815.

Matthews, Andrew - Recruit - 26th US Infantry - Recruiting Detachment: William Bezeau - Age: 30 - Height: 5' 5" - Eyes: Black - Hair: Curly - Complexion: Black - Born: Ohio - Trade: Seaman - Enlistment date: 9 Feb 1815 - Place: Philadelphia - Period: War - Enlisted by whom: William Bezeau - Listed on the Descriptive Roll of Colored Men, 1 Apr 1815.

Maxwell, Samuel - Recruit - 26th US Infantry - Recruiting Detachment: William Bezeau - Age: 19 - Height: 5' 6" - Eyes: Black - Hair: Curly - Complexion: Black - Born: Pennsylvania - Trade: Farmer - Enlistment date: 27 Jan 1815 - Place: Philadelphia - Period: War - Enlisted by whom: William Bezeau - Listed on the Descriptive Roll of Colored Men, 1 Apr 1815.

McCoy, Archibald - Private - 1st US Rifles - Company: Samuel Hamilton - Age: 25 - Height: 5' 8" - Eyes: Brown - Hair: Brown - Complexion: Brown - Born: Sussex County, NY - Trade: Farmer - Enlistment date: 24 Apr 1814 - Place: Easton, PA - Period: War - Enlisted by whom: Lodowick Morgan - Discharged at Plattsburg, NY, on 24 Aug 1815.

McIntire, Solomon - Recruit - 26th US Infantry - Recruiting Detachment: William Bezeau - Age: 23 - Height: 5' 8" - Eyes: Black - Hair: Curly - Complexion: Yellow - Born: New Jersey - Trade: Farmer - Enlistment date: 10 Nov 1814 - Place: Philadelphia - Period: War - Enlisted by whom: William Bezeau - BLW 7198-160-12 - Listed as "Col'd" in his service record; discharged at Philadelphia on 23 Mar 1815.

McMullen, Cyrus - Recruit - 26th US Infantry - Recruiting Detachment: William Bezeau - Age: 29 - Height: 5' 8" - Eyes: Black - Hair: Curly - Complexion: Black - Born: Louisiana - Trade: Seaman - Enlistment date: 3 Feb 1815 - Place: Philadelphia - Period: War - Enlisted by whom: William Bezeau - Listed on the Descriptive Roll of Colored Men, 1 Apr 1815.

McMutrie, Samuel - Recruit - 26th US Infantry - Recruiting Detachment: William Bezeau - Age: 36 - Height: 5' 10" - Eyes: Black - Hair: Black - Complexion: Brown - Born: New Jersey - Trade: Laborer - Enlistment date: 23 Oct 1814 - Place: Philadelphia - Period: War - Enlisted by whom: William Bezeau - BLW 7200-160-12 - Listed as "Col'd" in his service record; discharged at

Philadelphia on 23 Mar 1815.

Meirs, Shadrack - Recruit - 26th US Infantry - Recruiting Detachment: William Bezeau - Age: 15 - Height: 4' 6" - Eyes: Black - Hair: Black - Complexion: Black - Born: Pennsylvania - Trade: Laborer - Enlistment date: 11 Oct 1814 - Place: Philadelphia - Period: War - Enlisted by whom: William Bezeau - Listed as "Col'd" in his service record; discharged for being a minor.

Meldrom, James - Recruit - 26th US Infantry - Recruiting Detachment: William Bezeau - Age: 35 - Height: 5' 10 1/2" - Eyes: Black - Hair: Black - Complexion: Yellow - Born: New Jersey - Trade: Farmer - Enlistment date: 9 Oct 1814 - Place: Philadelphia - Period: 5 Yrs - Enlisted by whom: William Bezeau - Listed as "Col'd" in his service record; discharged at Philadelphia on 25 May 1815.

Melona, Cornelius - Laborer - Corps of Artificers - Company: Alexander Parris - Listed as "Black" in *A List of Pensioners of the War of 1812*.

Merry, Joseph (Meny) - Private - US Light Artillery - Company: John Bell - Age: 22 - Height: 5' 4" - Eyes: Black or Dark - Hair: Black or Dark - Complexion: Dark - Born: Havana, Cuba - Trade: Mariner - Enlistment date: 20 Jun 1814 - Place: Boston - Period: War - Enlisted by whom: Samuel Washburn - Discharged on 31 Mar 1815.

Midden, Joseph - Recruit - 26th US Infantry - Recruiting Detachment: William Bezeau - Age: 21 - Height: 6' - Eyes: Black - Hair: Curly - Complexion: Black - Born: Pennsylvania - Trade: Seaman - Enlistment date: 7 Feb 1815 - Place: Philadelphia - Period: War - Enlisted by whom: William Bezeau - Listed on the Descriptive Roll of Colored Men, 1 Apr 1815.

Milleman, Prince - Private - 30th US Infantry - Company: Sylvanus Danforth - Other regiment: US Light Artillery - Age: 36 - Height: 5' 8" - Eyes: Black - Hair: Curly - Complexion: Negro - Born: Newport, RI - Trade: Farmer - Enlistment date: 27 Oct 1814 - Place: Middlebury, VT - Period: 5 Yrs - Enlisted by whom: Simeon Wright - Transferred to the U.S. Light Artillery, Captain Nathan Towson's Company; deserted at Fort Warren, VT, on 2 Aug 1816.

Miller, Abraham - Private - 16th US Infantry - Company: Robert Gray - Age: 44 - Height: 5' 8" - Eyes: Black - Hair: Black - Complexion: Black - Born: Pennsylvania - Trade: Weaver - Enlistment date: 15 Sep 1812 - Place: Marietta, PA - Period: 5 Yrs - Enlisted by whom: Terah. Jones.

Miller, William - Recruit - 26th US Infantry - Recruiting Detachment: William Bezeau - Age: 22 - Height: 5' - Eyes: Black - Hair: Black - Complexion: Black or Dark - Born: Pennsylvania - Trade: Farmer - Enlistment date: 10 Sep 1814 - Place: Philadelphia - Period: 5 Yrs - Enlisted by whom: William Bezeau - Listed as a "Blackman" in his service record; discharged at Philadelphia on 22 May 1815.

Millet, John - Private - 27th US Infantry - Company: James Porter - Age: 32 - Height: 5' 6" - Eyes: Dark - Hair: Black - Complexion: Dark Colored - Born: San Domingo (Haiti) - Trade: Musician - Enlistment date: 30 Sep 1814 - Place: Hudson, NY - Period: 5 Yrs - Enlisted by whom: Maxwell - BLW 2762-160-12 - Discharged on 11 Aug 1815.

Millikin, James - Laborer - Corps of Artificers - Company: Alexander Parris - Listed as "Black" in *A List of Pensioners of the War of 1812*.

Minot, Samuel - Private - 31st US Infantry - Company: Ethan Burnap - Age: 22 - Height: 5' 9" - Eyes:

Black - Hair: Black - Complexion: Black - Born: Boston - Trade: Farmer - Enlistment date: 3 Mar 1814 - Place: Thetford or Montpelier, VT - Period: War - Enlisted by whom: John Hatch - Discharged on 4 Jun 1815 on a Surgeon's Certificate of Discharge.

Moasley, William - Private - 39th US Infantry - Company: George Hallum - Reported as a Negro; discharged on 9 Jan 1815.

Montgomery, John - Private - 13th US Infantry - Company: Mordecai Myers - Age: 34 - Height: 5' 8" - Eyes: Dark - Hair: Dark - Complexion: Black - Born: New Derry, VT - Trade: Farmer - Enlistment date: 29 Sep 1814 - Place: Auburn - Period: 5 Yrs - Enlisted by whom: Henry Minton.

Moore, John - Private - 31st US Infantry - Age: 21 - Height: 5' 5" - Eyes: Black - Hair: Black - Complexion: Black - Born: Londonderry, NH - Trade: Barber - Enlistment date: 18 Apr 1814 - Place: Pomfret or Thetford, VT - Period: War - Enlisted by whom: Amos Brown - Died on 8 Dec 1814.

Moore, John - Recruit - 26th US Infantry - Recruiting Detachment: William Bezeau - Age: 30 - Height: 5' - Eyes: Black - Hair: Black - Complexion: Black - Born: Philadelphia - Trade: Blacksmith - Enlistment date: 10 Sep 1814 - Place: Philadelphia - Period: 5 Yrs - Enlisted by whom: William Bezeau - Listed as "Col'd" in his service record; discharged at Philadelphia on 20 May 1815.

Moore, Samuel (Moores) - Private - US Light Artillery - Company: George Morris - Age: 21 - Height: 5' 6" - Eyes: Black - Hair: Black - Complexion: Black - Born: Lanesborough, MA - Enlistment date: 15 Jul 1814 - Place: Boston - Period: War - Enlisted by whom: Samuel Washburn - Absent 16 Feb 1815, left sick at Plattsburg, NY, supposed to be at Sackets Harbor, NY.

Moore, Silas - Private - 4th US Infantry - Company: Ebenezer Way - Age: 21 - Height: 5' - Eyes: Black - Hair: Black - Complexion: Black - Born: Dumbarton, NH - Trade: Laborer - Enlistment date: 4 Oct 1814 - Period: War - Enlisted by whom: Lieutenant Low - Discharged at Portsmouth, NH, on 1 Apr 1815.

Morris, Moses - Private - 14th US Infantry - Company: David Cummings - Age: 19 - Height: 5' 5" - Eyes: Dark - Hair: Black - Complexion: Yellow - Born: Loudoun County, VA - Trade: Brick maker - Enlistment date: 6 Nov 1814 - Place: Snowden Camp - Period: 5 Yrs - Enlisted by whom: Lieutenant Riddle - Deserted at Fort McHenry, MD, on 15 Apr 1815.

Morris, Samuel - Recruit - 26th US Infantry - Recruiting Detachment: William Bezeau - Age: 39 - Height: 5' 5" - Eyes: Black - Hair: Curly - Complexion: Black - Born: Lancaster County, PA - Trade: Sailor - Enlistment date: 10 Oct 1814 - Place: Philadelphia - Period: 5 Yrs - Enlisted by whom: William Bezeau - Listed as "Col'd" in his service record; discharged at Philadelphia on 20 May 1815.

Morton, Isaac - Recruit - 26th US Infantry - Recruiting Detachment: William Bezeau - Age: 34 - Height: 5' 9" - Eyes: Black - Hair: Curly - Complexion: Black - Born: Pennsylvania - Trade: Farmer - Enlistment date: 11 Feb 1815 - Place: Philadelphia - Period: War - Enlisted by whom: William Bezeau.

Munn, Edward - Recruit - 26th US Infantry - Recruiting Detachment: William Bezeau - Age: 22 - Height: 5' 10" - Eyes: Black - Hair: Curly - Complexion: Black - Born: Pennsylvania - Trade: Farmer - Enlistment date: 23 Jan 1815 - Place: Philadelphia - Period: War - Enlisted by whom: William Bezeau - Listed on the Descriptive Roll of Colored Men, 1 Apr 1815; deserted on 27 Jan 1815.

Nahn, John - Recruit - 26th US Infantry - Recruiting Detachment: William Bezeau - Age: 21 - Height: 5' 3 1/2" - Eyes: Black - Hair: Curly - Complexion: Black - Born: Africa - Trade: Laborer - Enlistment date: 21 Nov 1814 - Place: Philadelphia - Period: War - Enlisted by whom: William Bezeau - Listed as "Col'd" in his service record; deserted on 22 Nov 1814.

Nelson, Isaac - Musician - US Light Artillery - Company: George Morris - Age: 21 - Height: 5' 5" - Eyes: Black - Hair: Black - Complexion: Black - Born: Albany County, NY - Trade: Farmer - Enlistment date: 8 Sep 1814 - Place: Boston - Period: War - Enlisted by whom: Samuel Washburn - Discharged on 31 Mar 1815.

Nelson, John - Private - 2nd US Artillery - Company: Philemon Hawkins - Age: 22 - Height: 6' 2" - Eyes: Black - Hair: Dark - Complexion: Dark - Born: West Indies - Trade: Carpenter - Enlistment date: 11 Dec 1814 - Period: War - Enlisted by whom: Lieutenant Guy.

Nelson, Robert H. - Private - US Light Artillery - Company: Samuel Spotts - Age: 31 - Height: 6' - Eyes: Grey - Hair: Brown - Complexion: Black - Born: New York - Trade: Farmer - Enlistment date: 22 Mar 1813 - Place: New Orleans - Period: War - Enlisted by whom: Samuel Spotts - Discharged on 9 Apr 1815.

Newburn, John - Recruit - 26th US Infantry - Recruiting Detachment: William Bezeau - Age: 28 - Height: 5' 9" - Eyes: Black - Hair: Curly - Complexion: Black - Born: Pennsylvania - Trade: Laborer - Enlistment date: 17 Jan 1815 - Place: Philadelphia - Period: War - Enlisted by whom: William Bezeau - Listed on the Descriptive Roll of Colored Men, 1 Apr 1815.

Nichols, Samuel - Recruit - 26th US Infantry - Recruiting Detachment: William Bezeau - Age: 28 - Height: 5' 7" - Eyes: Black - Hair: Curly - Complexion: Brown - Born: Virginia - Trade: Laborer - Enlistment date: 1 Jan 1815 - Period: War - BLW 537-320-14 - Discharged at Philadelphia.

Nixon, Richard - Recruit - 26th US Infantry - Recruiting Detachment: William Bezeau - Age: 25 - Height: 5' - Eyes: Black - Hair: Curly - Complexion: Chestnut - Born: New York - Trade: Laborer - Enlistment date: 2 Nov 1814 - Place: Philadelphia - Period: War - Enlisted by whom: William Bezeau - BLW 7289-160-12 - Listed as "Col'd" in his service record; discharged at Philadelphia on 20 Mar 1815.

Noble, Jordan B. - Musician - 7th US Infantry - Pension: SO-22074, SC-19527, IO-408304; served as a musician in the 7th US Infantry (War of 1812), in Colonel P. F. Smith's Louisiana Volunteers (Florida War of 1836), in Colonel Watrous' Louisiana Volunteers (Mexican War), and as a captain of Company C, Louisiana Volunteers (Civil War) - BLW 30300-160-55 (Mexican War Service) - Service record for the War of 1812 has not been found; received pension for Mexican War service.

Nopley, George - Recruit - 26th US Infantry - Recruiting Detachment: William Bezeau - Age: 34 - Height: 6' - Eyes: Black - Hair: Curly - Complexion: Brown - Born: Pennsylvania - Trade: Laborer - Enlistment date: 20 Jan 1815 - Place: Philadelphia - Period: War - Enlisted by whom: William Bezeau - Listed on the Descriptive Roll of Colored Men, 1 Apr 1815.

Norlin, Luke - Recruit - 26th US Infantry - Recruiting Detachment: William Bezeau - Age: 35 - Height: 5' 7" - Eyes: Black - Hair: Curly - Complexion: Black - Born: Pennsylvania - Trade: Laborer - Enlistment date: 16 Jan 1815 - Place: Philadelphia - Period: War - Enlisted by whom: William Bezeau - Listed on the Descriptive Roll of Colored Men, 1 Apr 1815.

Obman, Edward - Recruit - 26th US Infantry - Recruiting Detachment: William Bezeau - Age: 30 - Height: 5' 7" - Eyes: Black - Hair: Curly - Complexion: Black - Born: Pennsylvania - Trade: Laborer - Enlistment date: 22 Jan 1815 - Place: Philadelphia - Period: War - Enlisted by whom: William Bezeau - Listed on the Descriptive Roll of Colored Men, 1 Apr 1815; deserted on 27 Jan 1815.

Olden, Seth - Recruit - 26th US Infantry - Recruiting Detachment: William Bezeau - Age: 19 - Height: 5' 5" - Eyes: Black - Hair: Black - Complexion: Black - Born: Philadelphia - Trade: Laborer - Enlistment date: 3 Sep 1814 - Place: Philadelphia - Period: 5 Yrs - Enlisted by whom: William Bezeau - Listed as "Col'd" in his service record; discharged at Philadelphia on 16 May 1815.

Orteza, Dominic - Musician - 5th US Infantry - Company: James Dorman - Height: 5' 4" - Eyes: Black - Hair: Black - Complexion: Black - Born: Italy - Trade: Musician - Enlistment date: 1 May 1811 - Place: Georgetown, DC - Period: 5 Yrs - Enlisted by whom: J. Johnson.

Oston, Charles - Recruit - 26th US Infantry - Recruiting Detachment: William Bezeau - Age: 24 - Height: 5' 6" - Eyes: Black - Hair: Curly - Complexion: Black - Born: Pennsylvania - Trade: Laborer - Enlistment date: 4 Jan 1815 - Place: Philadelphia - Period: War - Enlisted by whom: William Bezeau - Listed on the Descriptive Roll of Colored Men, 1 Apr 1815.

Ostrander, Harry - Private - 29th US Infantry - Company: Mathew Danvers - Age: 23 - Height: 5' 7 1/2" - Eyes: Black - Hair: Black - Complexion: Yellow - Born: Waterfleet, NY - Trade: Laborer - Enlistment date: 8 Dec 1814 - Place: Troy, NY - Period: War - Enlisted by whom: Thomas Vail - Discharged at Champlain, NY, on 29 Jun 1815.

Page, Sampson - Private - US Light Artillery - Company: John McIntosh - Age: 29 - Height: 5' 3 1/2" - Eyes: Black - Hair: Black - Complexion: Black - Born: Dumbarton, NH - Trade: Farmer - Enlistment date: 20 Jul 1814 - Place: Boston - Period: War - Enlisted by whom: Samuel Washburn - Discharged at Plattsburgh, NY, on 31 May 1815.

Painter, William - Recruit - 26th US Infantry - Recruiting Detachment: William Bezeau - Age: 24 - Height: 5' 4" - Eyes: Black - Hair: Curly - Complexion: Yellow - Born: Pennsylvania - Trade: Seaman - Enlistment date: 3 Jan 1815 - Place: Philadelphia - Period: War - Enlisted by whom: William Bezeau - Listed on the Descriptive Roll of Colored Men, 1 Apr 1815.

Palmer, Jacob - Private - 31st US Infantry - Company: Rufus Stewart - Age: 24 - Height: 5' 11" - Eyes: Black - Hair: Black - Complexion: Black - Born: Stonington, CT - Trade: Farmer - Enlistment date: 22 Feb 1814 - Place: Plattsburgh, NY - Period: War - Enlisted by whom: Ethan Burnap - Deserted from Plattsburg, NY, on 9 Jul 1814.

Palmer, John - Recruit - 26th US Infantry - Recruiting Detachment: William Bezeau - Age: 29 - Height: 5' 6" - Eyes: Black - Hair: Curly - Complexion: Brown - Born: New Jersey - Trade: Laborer - Enlistment date: 20 Nov 1814 - Place: Philadelphia - Period: War - Enlisted by whom: William Bezeau - BLW 7204-160-12 - Listed as "Colored" in his service record; discharged at Philadelphia on 20 Mar 1815.

Parcels, Isaac - Private - US Light Artillery - Company: Jonathan Brooks - Age: 25 - Height: 5' 10" - Eyes: Black - Hair: Black - Complexion: Black - Born: South or Turtle Bay, NY - Trade: Carpenter - Enlistment date: 4 Dec 1812 - Place: New York - Period: 5 Yrs - Enlisted by whom: Jonathan Brooks - Discharged on 4 Dec 1817.

Ransalier – see John Rensellar

Parker, John - Recruit - 26th US Infantry - Recruiting Detachment: William Bezeau - Age: 25 - Height: 5' 9" - Born: Pennsylvania - Enlistment date: 21 Sep 1814 - Place: Philadelphia - Enlisted by whom: William Bezeau - Listed as "Colored" in his service record; deserted on 28 Sep 1814.

Parrish, John - Private - 8th US Infantry - Company: William Chisolm - Other regiment: 7th US Infantry - Age: 18 - Height: 5' 8 1/2" - Eyes: Black - Hair: Dark - Complexion: Yellow - Born: Columbia, GA - Trade: Farmer - Enlistment date: 6 Oct 1812 - Place: Watkinsville - Period: 5 Yrs - Enlisted by whom: Lieutenant Mallry - BLW 19148-160-12 - Discharged at Fort Crawford, IL, on 6 Oct 1817.

Paskal, John - Recruit - 26th US Infantry - Recruiting Detachment: William Bezeau - Age: 28 - Height: 5' 5" - Eyes: Black - Hair: Curly - Complexion: Black - Born: Delaware - Trade: Sailor - Enlistment date: 2 Nov 1814 - Place: Philadelphia - Period: War - Enlisted by whom: William Bezeau - BLW 10290-160-12 - Listed as "Col'd" in his service record; discharged at Philadelphia on 20 Mar 1815.

Paul, John - Private - US Light Artillery - Company: John McIntosh - Age: 23 - Height: 5' 6" - Eyes: Black - Hair: Black - Complexion: Black - Born: New Orleans - Trade: Mariner - Enlistment date: 15 Jul 1814 - Place: Boston - Period: War - Enlisted by whom: Samuel Washburn - Absent 16 Feb 1815, left sick at Plattsburg, NY, supposed to be at Sackets Harbor, NY.

Perry, James - Private - US Light Artillery - Company: John Bell - Age: 18 - Height: 5' 6" - Eyes: Black - Hair: Black - Complexion: Black - Born: Boston, Baltimore or Queen Ann County - Trade: Mariner - Enlistment date: 3 Nov 1814 - Place: Concord or Boston, MA - Period: 5 Yrs - Enlisted by whom: Richard Field - Discharged on 31 Mar 1815 on account of being a Negro and not a fit companion for the American soldier.

Peters, Jacob - Recruit - 26th US Infantry - Recruiting Detachment: William Bezeau - Age: 36 - Height: 5' 5" - Eyes: Dark - Hair: Dark - Complexion: Dark - Born: Pennsylvania - Trade: Laborer - Enlistment date: 22 Nov 1814 - Place: Philadelphia - Enlisted by whom: William Bezeau - BLW 18555-160-12 - Listed as "Colored" in his service record; discharged at Philadelphia on 20 Mar 1815.

Peters, John - Recruit - 26th US Infantry - Recruiting Detachment: William Bezeau - Age: 30 - Height: 5' 7" - Eyes: Black - Hair: Black - Complexion: Black - Born: San Domingo (Haiti) - Trade: Cook - Enlistment date: 22 Nov 1814 - Place: Philadelphia - Period: 5 Yrs - Enlisted by whom: William Bezeau - Listed on the Descriptive Roll of Negroes, 25 May 1815 and as "Colored" in his service record; discharged at Philadelphia on 20 Mar 1815.

Peters, Scipio - Recruit - 26th US Infantry - Recruiting Detachment: William Bezeau - Age: 40 - Height: 5' 7" - Born: Philadelphia - Enlistment date: 24 Nov 1814 - Place: Philadelphia - Period: 5 Yrs - Enlisted by whom: William Bezeau - Listed as "Colored" in his service record; deserted on 10 Dec 1814.

Phillips, George - Recruit - 26th US Infantry - Recruiting Detachment: William Bezeau - Age: 30 - Height: 5' 7" - Eyes: Black - Hair: Black - Complexion: Black - Born: Pennsylvania - Trade: Laborer - Enlistment date: 31 Oct 1814 - Place: Philadelphia - Period: 5 Yrs - Enlisted by whom: William Bezeau - Listed as a "Colored man" in his service record; discharged at Philadelphia on 1 May 1815.

Phillips, George - Private - US Light Artillery - Company: George Morris - Age: 26 - Height: 5' 6 1/2" -

Eyes: Black - Hair: Black - Complexion: Black - Born: Boston or Lexington, MA - Trade: Farmer - Enlistment date: 3 Oct 1814 - Place: Boston - Period: War - Enlisted by whom: William Campbell - Discharged on 31 Mar 1815.

Phillips, Isaac - Recruit - 26th US Infantry - Recruiting Detachment: William Bezeau - Age: 22 - Height: 5' 5 1/2" - Eyes: Hazel - Hair: Curly - Complexion: Yellow - Born: Pennsylvania - Trade: Tobacconist - Enlistment date: 5 Nov 1814 - Place: Philadelphia - Period: War - Enlisted by whom: William Bezeau - BLW 14820-160-12 - Listed as "Colored" in his service record; discharged at Philadelphia on 23 Mar 1815.

Pierce, James - Recruit - 26th US Infantry - Recruiting Detachment: William Bezeau - Age: 20 - Height: 5' 7 1/2" - Born: Delaware - Enlistment date: 23 Nov 1814 - Place: Philadelphia - Period: 5 Yrs - Enlisted by whom: William Bezeau - Listed as "Colored" in his service record; given up to the Navy in Jan 1815, a deserter.

Pierce, Lewis - Recruit - 26th US Infantry - Recruiting Detachment: William Bezeau - Age: 20 - Height: 5' 2" - Eyes: Black - Hair: Curly - Complexion: Black - Born: Pennsylvania - Trade: Laborer - Enlistment date: 8 Feb 1815 - Place: Philadelphia - Period: War - Enlisted by whom: William Bezeau - Listed on the Descriptive Roll of Colored Men, 1 Apr 1815.

Pitts, Jesse - Private - 8th US Infantry - Company: Thomas Farrar - Age: 23 - Height: 5' 9 1/4" - Eyes: Black - Hair: Black - Complexion: Brown - Born: Barnwell County, SC - Trade: Farmer - Enlistment date: 11 Aug 1814 - Place: Camp Flourney, GA - Period: 5 Yrs - Enlisted by whom: William Bee.

Plaine, Samuel - Recruit Corporal - 26th US Infantry - Recruiting Detachment: William Bezeau - Age: 22 - Height: 5' 9 1/2" - Eyes: Brown - Hair: Brown - Complexion: Brown - Born: Pennsylvania - Trade: Cooper - Enlistment date: 8 Sep 1814 - Place: Philadelphia - Period: War - Enlisted by whom: William Bezeau - BLW 10297-160-42 - Discharged at Philadelphia on 23 Mar 1815.

Pomroy, William - Recruit - 26th US Infantry - Recruiting Detachment: William Bezeau - Age: 32 - Height: 5' 3" - Eyes: Black - Hair: Curly - Complexion: Black - Born: Pennsylvania - Trade: Farmer - Enlistment date: 7 Jan 1814 - Place: Philadelphia - Period: War - Enlisted by whom: William Bezeau - Listed on the Descriptive Roll of Colored Men, 1 Apr 1815.

Porter, John - Private - 21st US Infantry - Company: Morrill Marston - Age: 39 - Height: 5' 6 1/2" - Eyes: Hazel - Hair: Black - Complexion: Black - Born: Germany - Trade: Mariner - Enlistment date: 30 May 1814 - Place: Portsmouth, NH - Period: 5 Yrs - Enlisted by whom: John Dix - Died in Brownsville, NY, on 20 Apr 1815.

Portland, Thomas - Recruit - 26th US Infantry - Recruiting Detachment: William Bezeau - Age: 17 - Height: 4' 8" - Eyes: Brown - Hair: Curly - Complexion: Sambo - Born: New Jersey - Trade: Waiter - Enlistment date: 4 Dec 1814 - Period: War - Enlisted by whom: William Bezeau - BLW 5889-160-12 - Listed as "Colored" in his service record, discharged at Philadelphia on 20 Mar 1815.

Prentis, Leonard (Prentice) - Private - US Light Artillery - Company: George Morris - Age: 21 - Height: 5' 5 3/4" - Eyes: Black - Hair: Black or Dark - Complexion: Black - Born: Londonderry, NH - Trade: Mariner - Enlistment date: 18 Jul 1814 - Place: Boston - Period: War - Enlisted by whom: Samuel Washburn - Discharged on 31 Mar 1815.

Pullard, Jacob - Recruit - 26th US Infantry - Recruiting Detachment: William Bezeau - Age: 22 - Height: 5' 6" - Eyes: Black - Hair: Curly - Complexion: Black - Born: Pennsylvania - Trade: Laborer - Enlistment date: 15 Jan 1815 - Place: Philadelphia - Period: War - Enlisted by whom: William Bezeau - Listed on the Descriptive Roll of Colored Men, 1 Apr 1815.

Pursue, Aaron - Recruit - 26th US Infantry - Recruiting Detachment: William Bezeau - Age: 32 - Height: 5' - Eyes: Hazel - Hair: Curly - Complexion: Yellow - Born: New Jersey - Trade: Laborer - Enlistment date: 14 Oct 1814 - Place: Philadelphia - Period: War - Enlisted by whom: William Bezeau - BLW 17203-160-42 - Listed as "Col'd" in his service record; discharged at Philadelphia on 23 Mar 1815.

Ramsey, Joseph - Recruit - 26th US Infantry - Recruiting Detachment: William Bezeau - Age: 17 - Height: 5' 4" - Eyes: Curly - Hair: Curly - Complexion: Black - Born: Pennsylvania - Trade: Laborer - Enlistment date: 2 Feb 1815 - Place: Philadelphia - Period: War - Enlisted by whom: William Bezeau - Listed on the Descriptive Roll of Colored Men, 1 Apr 1815.

Rensellar, John - Private - 11th US Infantry - Company: Benjamin Smead - Age: 26 - Height: 5' 6" - Eyes: Black - Hair: Black - Complexion: Black - Trade: Farmer - Enlistment date: 4 Mar 1813 - Period: 5 Yrs - Listed as a "Blackman" in his service record; American prisoner of war at Halifax, NS (no further information found).

Richardson, John - Recruit - 26th US Infantry - Recruiting Detachment: William Bezeau - Age: 27 - Height: 5' 10 1/2" - Eyes: Black - Hair: Black - Complexion: Yellow - Born: Virginia - Trade: Laborer - Enlistment date: 1 Nov 1814 - Place: Philadelphia - Period: War - Enlisted by whom: William Bezeau - BLW 7291-120-12 - Listed as "Col'd" in his service record; discharged at Philadelphia on 22 Mar 1815.

Ridgeway, Samuel - Laborer - Corps of Artificers - Company: Alexander Parris - Listed as "Black" in *A List of Pensioners of the War of 1812*.

Roberts, John - Private - 8th US Infantry - Company: John Allison - Other regiment: 7th US Infantry - Age: 26 - Height: 5' 10 1/2" - Eyes: Black - Hair: Black - Complexion: Black - Born: Charlotte, VA - Trade: Carpenter - Enlistment date: 4 Oct 1814 - Place: Fort Hawkins, GA - Period: 5 Yrs - Enlisted by whom: Lieutenant Womack - Deserted at Fort Hawkins, GA, on 1 May 1816.

Roberts, Thomas - Recruit - 26th US Infantry - Recruiting Detachment: William Bezeau - Age: 19 - Height: 5' 3" - Eyes: Black - Hair: Curly - Complexion: Black - Born: Pennsylvania - Trade: Laborer - Enlistment date: 17 Jan 1815 - Place: Philadelphia - Period: War - Enlisted by whom: William Bezeau - Listed on the Descriptive Roll of Colored Men, 1 Apr 1815.

Robinson, George (Robertson) - Private - US Light Artillery - Company: George Morris - Age: 28 - Height: 5' 5 3/4" - Eyes: Black - Hair: Black - Complexion: Black - Born: Accomack County, VA - Trade: Mariner - Enlistment date: 6 Oct 1814 - Place: Boston - Period: War - Enlisted by whom: William Campbell.

Robinson, Simon (Robertson) - Private - US Light Artillery - Company: George Morris - Age: 32 - Height: 6' - Eyes: Black - Hair: Black - Complexion: Black or Dark - Born: New Jersey - Trade: Farmer - Enlistment date: 1 Aug 1814 - Place: Boston - Period: War - Enlisted by whom: Samuel Washburn - Discharged on 31 Mar 1815.

Robinson, William - Musician - 45th US Infantry - Company: Joshua Danforth - Age: 23 - Height: 5' 8

1/4" - Eyes: Black - Hair: Black - Complexion: Black - Born: Exeter, NH - Trade: Farmer - Enlistment date: 7 Apr 1814 - Place: Concord, NH - Period: War - Enlisted by whom: Lieutenant Low - Re-enlisted on 13 Mar 1815 for five years.

Rutter, Stephen - Private - US Light Artillery - Company: John McIntosh - Age: 29 - Height: 5' 5" - Eyes: Black - Hair: Black - Complexion: Black - Born: Philadelphia - Trade: Mariner - Enlistment date: 11 Jul 1814 - Place: Boston - Period: War - Enlisted by whom: Samuel Washburn – Dishonorable discharged at Plattsburg, NY, on 31 May 1815.

Sanderson, James - Recruit - 26th US Infantry - Recruiting Detachment: William Bezeau - Age: 22 - Height: 5' 11" - Eyes: Black - Hair: Curly - Complexion: Chestnut - Born: New Jersey - Trade: Laborer - Enlistment date: 3 Nov 1814 - Place: Philadelphia - Period: War - Enlisted by whom: William Bezeau - Listed as "Col'd" in his service record.

Sawyer, Nathaniel - Laborer - Corps of Artificers - Company: Alexander Parris - Listed as "Black" in *A List of Pensioners of the War of 1812.*

Scaudling, Jacob - Private - 38th US Infantry - Company: John Rothrock - Age: 27 - Height: 5' 11" - Eyes: Dark - Hair: Black - Complexion: Black - Born: Chester County, PA - Trade: Farmer - Enlistment date: 10 Aug 1813 - Place: Craney Island, VA - Period: War - Enlisted by whom: John Rothrock - Discharged at Craney Island, VA, on 15 Mar 1815.

Scott, Francis - Private - 39th US Infantry - Company: George Hallum - Enlistment date: 23 Jan 1814 - Reported as a Negro; discharged on 22 Jan 1815.

Scott, Wade - Private - 24th US Infantry - Company: James Campbell - Age: 35 - Height: 5' 10" - Eyes: Yellow - Hair: Curly - Complexion: Yellow - Born: Virginia - Trade: Farmer - Enlistment date: 20 Jan 1813 - Place: Wilson County, TN - Period: 5 Yrs - Enlisted by whom: Abner Haynes - List as a "Negro."

Scriver, John - Private - 23rd US Infantry - Company: Horatio Armstrong - Age: 21 - Height: 5' 3" - Eyes: Black - Hair: Black - Complexion: Black - Born: Sopus, KY - Trade: Blacksmith - Enlistment date: 4 Feb 1813 - Place: Rhinebeck, NY - Period: 5 Yrs - Enlisted by whom: Horatio Armstrong - Discharged on 5 Nov 1817 and re-enlisted.

Seamore, John - Recruit - US Light Artillery - Age: 21 - Height: 5' 2" - Born: Africa - Enlistment date: 18 Jul 1814 - Place: Boston - Enlisted by whom: Samuel Washburn.

Shanklin, Myers (or Mayer Shanklin) - Recruit - 26th US Infantry - Recruiting Detachment: William Bezeau - Age: 18 - Height: 5' 6" - Eyes: Black - Hair: Curly - Complexion: Black - Born: Pennsylvania - Trade: Rope maker - Enlistment date: 28 Dec 1814 - Place: Philadelphia - Period: 5 Yrs - Enlisted by whom: William Bezeau - Listed on the Descriptive Roll of Negroes, 25 May 1815 and as "Col'd" in his service record; discharged at Philadelphia on 22 May 1815.

Sharp, Solomon - Private - 11th US Infantry - Company: Benjamin Smead - Other regiment: 6th US Infantry - Age: 29 - Height: 5' 10" - Eyes: Black - Hair: Black - Complexion: Black - Born: Conway, MA - Trade: Farmer - Enlistment date: 2 Feb 1812 - Place: Bennington, VT - Period: 5 Yrs - Enlisted by whom: Benjamin Smead - BLW 16170-160-42 - Prisoner of War captured on 3 Jun 1813 on the US Sloop Growler on Lake Champlain, exchanged at Chazy, 11 May 1814; discharged on 2 Feb 1818.

Sherbourne, William - Private - US Light Artillery - Company: John McIntosh - Age: 29 - Height: 5' 6 1/2" - Eyes: Black - Hair: Black - Complexion: Black - Born: Londonderry, NH - Trade: Mariner - Enlistment date: 17 Jul 1814 - Place: Boston - Period: War - Enlisted by whom: Samuel Washburn - BLW 13924-160-12 - Discharged at Sackets Harbor, NY, on 25 May 1815.

Simmons, John - Private - US Light Artillery - Company: George Morris - Age: 23 - Height: 5' 6 1/2" - Eyes: Black - Hair: Black - Complexion: Black - Born: Bermuda - Trade: Mariner - Enlistment date: 8 Oct 1814 - Place: Boston - Period: War - Enlisted by whom: William Campbell - Discharged on 31 Mar 1815.

Simpson, Peter - Private - 23rd US Infantry - Company: Justus Ingersoll - Age: 24 - Height: 5' 6" - Eyes: Mulatto - Hair: Mulatto - Complexion: Mulatto - Born: Brookfield, CT - Trade: Shoemaker - Enlistment date: 7 Jan 1814 - Place: Batstown - Period: 5 Yrs - Enlisted by whom: Richard Smyth - BLW 9594-160-42 - Listed as a "Mulatto" in his service record; wounded at Fort Erie, UC; discharged at Sackets Harbor, NY, on 8 Jan 1815.

Smith, John - Recruit - 26th US Infantry - Recruiting Detachment: William Bezeau - Age: 24 - Height: 5' 6" - Eyes: Black - Hair: Curly - Complexion: Black - Born: New Jersey - Trade: Laborer - Enlistment date: 1 Jan 1815 - Place: Philadelphia - Period: 5 Yrs - Enlisted by whom: William Bezeau - Listed as a "Blackman" in his service record; discharged at Philadelphia on 1 May 1815.

Smith, Solomon - Recruit - 26th US Infantry - Recruiting Detachment: William Bezeau - Age: 33 - Height: 5' 9" - Eyes: Black - Hair: Black - Complexion: Black - Born: Delaware - Trade: Laborer - Enlistment date: 30 Nov 1814 - Place: Philadelphia - Period: 5 Yrs - Enlisted by whom: William Bezeau - Listed as a "Colored man" in his service record; discharged on 20 May 1815.

Smith, Thomas P. - Private - 23rd US Infantry - Company: Azariah Odell - Other regiment: 2nd US Infantry - Age: 38 - Height: 5' 8" - Eyes: Black - Hair: Black - Complexion: Black - Born: Pittsburgh, PA - Trade: Sawyer - Enlistment date: 27 Jun 1814 - Place: Albany, NY - Period: War - Enlisted by whom: William Clarke - Discharged on 5 Jun 1815.

Smith, William - Recruit - 26th US Infantry - Recruiting Detachment: William Bezeau - Age: 22 - Height: 5' 5" - Eyes: Black - Hair: Curly or Black - Complexion: Yellow - Born: Pennsylvania - Trade: Farmer - Enlistment date: 11 Nov 1814 - Place: Philadelphia - Period: 5 Yrs - Enlisted by whom: William Bezeau - Listed on the Descriptive Roll of Negroes, 25 May 1815 and as "Col'd" in his service record; discharged at Philadelphia on 17 May 1815.

Spanason, John - Recruit - 26th US Infantry - Recruiting Detachment: William Bezeau - Age: 22 - Height: 5' 10" - Eyes: Black - Hair: Curly - Complexion: Brown - Born: Philadelphia - Trade: Laborer - Enlistment date: 21 Nov 1814 - Place: Philadelphia - Period: War - Enlisted by whom: William Bezeau - Listed as "Col'd" in his service record.

Spencer, Benjamin - Recruit - 26th US Infantry - Recruiting Detachment: William Bezeau - Age: 28 - Height: 5' 5" - Eyes: Black - Hair: Curly - Complexion: Black - Born: Delaware - Trade: Laborer - Enlistment date: 3 Jan 1815 - Place: Philadelphia - Period: War - Enlisted by whom: William Bezeau - Pension: Land bounty to Isaac Spencer, cousin & only heir at law of Benjamin Spencer, deceased; died before 6 Jul 1819; first land bounty cancelled by an order from the War Department on 19 May 1820 - BLW 812-320-14 Cancelled; BLW 1038-320-14 - Listed on the Descriptive Roll of Colored Men, 1 Apr 1815.

Springsteen, John - Private - 41st US Infantry - Company: Mangle Quackenbos - Age: 29 - Height: 5' 9" -

Eyes: Black - Hair: Dark - Complexion: Black - Born: Poughkeepsie, NY - Trade: Shoemaker - Enlistment date: 25 Aug 1814 - Place: Hudson, NY - Period: War - Enlisted by whom: Theophilius Beekman - Deserted on 24 Apr 1815.

Stanley, Samuel - Private - 11th US Infantry - Company: Horace Hale - Age: 15 - Height: 5' 7 1/2" - Eyes: Black - Hair: Black - Complexion: Black - Born: Shapley, MA - Trade: Farmer - Enlistment date: 6 Feb 1813 - Place: Pottersfield - Period: 18 Mos - Enlisted by whom: Jonathan Stark - Discharged at Fort Erie, UC, on 10 Aug 1814.

Stewart, John - Private - 25th US Infantry - Company: Joseph Kinney - Age: 20 - Height: 5' 10" - Eyes: Black - Hair: Black - Complexion: Mulatto - Trade: Farmer - Enlistment date: 5 Feb 1813 - Place: Windsor, CT - Period: War - Enlisted by whom: Ensign Hill - Deserted at Sackets Harbor, NY, on 29 Oct 1813.

Stratten, Isaac (Statten) - Recruit - 26th US Infantry - Recruiting Detachment: William Bezeau - Age: 26 - Height: 5' 5" - Eyes: Black - Hair: Black - Complexion: Black - Born: New Jersey - Trade: Shoemaker - Enlistment date: 21 Sep 1814 - Place: Philadelphia - Period: 5 Yrs - Enlisted by whom: William Bezeau - Listed on the Descriptive Roll of Negroes, 25 May 1815 and as "Col'd" in his service record; discharged on 25 May 1815.

Shurbarn – See William Sherbourne

Sutton, Dempsey - Private - 24th US Infantry - Company: James Campbell - Other regiment: 7th US Infantry - Age: 26 - Height: 5' 10" - Eyes: Black - Hair: Black - Complexion: Yellow - Born: North Carolina - Trade: Farmer - Enlistment date: 13 Dec 1813 - Place: Wilson County, TN - Period: 5 Yrs - Enlisted by whom: Hays - Discharged at Fort Gadsen, FL, on 13 Dec 1818.

Tallsbury, Caesar (Tallsberry) - Private - US Light Artillery - Company: George Morris - Age: 19 - Height: 5' 3" - Eyes: Black - Hair: Black - Complexion: Black - Born: Coventry, RI - Trade: Laborer - Enlistment date: 29 Jul 1814 - Place: Providence or Dedham, RI - Period: War - Enlisted by whom: William Campbell - Listed as "Blk" in his service record; discharged on 31 Mar 1815.

Taylor, Isaac - Recruit - 26th US Infantry - Recruiting Detachment: William Bezeau - Age: 24 - Height: 5' 6" - Eyes: Black - Hair: Curly - Complexion: Brown - Born: Delaware - Trade: Farmer - Enlistment date: 27 Jan 1815 - Place: Philadelphia - Period: War - Enlisted by whom: William Bezeau - Listed on the Descriptive Roll of Colored Men, 1 Apr 1815.

Taylor, Julius C. - Recruit Sergeant - 26th US Infantry - Recruiting Detachment: William Bezeau - Age: 32 - Height: 6' - Eyes: Grey - Hair: Brown - Complexion: Fair or Light - Born: Columbia County, NY - Trade: Farmer - Enlistment date: 12 Feb 1815 - Period: War - Enlisted by whom: William Bezeau - BLW 212-320-14 - Listed as "Col'd" in his service record; discharged at Philadelphia on 30 May 1815.

Thomas, Benjamin - Private - 15th US Infantry - Company: Zachariah Rossell - Other regiment: Corps of Artillery - Age: 25 - Height: 5' 9 1/2" - Eyes: Black - Hair: Black - Complexion: Copper - Born: Bucks County, PA - Trade: Basket maker - Enlistment date: 17 Jun 1812 - Place: Mount Holly, NJ - Period: 5 Yrs - Enlisted by whom: Lieutenant Barton - Transferred to U.S. Corps of Artillery; re-enlisted in 1817.

Thomas, James - Recruit - 26th US Infantry - Recruiting Detachment: William Bezeau - Age: 17 - Height: 5' 4" - Eyes: Black - Hair: Curly - Complexion: Dark - Born: Pennsylvania - Trade: Laborer -

Enlistment date: 16 Nov 1814 - Place: Philadelphia - Period: War - Enlisted by whom: William Bezeau - BLW 10298-160-12 - Listed as "Col'd" in his service record; discharged at Philadelphia on 20 Mar 1815.

Thomas, Jeremiah - Sergeant - 16th US Infantry - Company: W. M. Oliver - Age: 23 - Height: 5' 8" - Eyes: Brown - Hair: Black - Complexion: Yellow - Born: Pennsylvania - Enlistment date: 23 Oct 1813 - Place: Carlisle, PA - Period: War - Enlisted by whom: William Downey - Discharged at Buffalo, NY, on 1 Jun 1815.

Thomas, Robert - Laborer - Corps of Artificers - Company: Alexander Parris - Listed as "Black" in *A List of Pensioners of the War of 1812.*

Thompson, Francis - Private - 11th US Infantry - Company: William Foster - Age: 21 - Height: 5' 8" - Eyes: Black - Hair: Black - Complexion: Black - Born: Bethlehem, NY - Trade: Farmer - Enlistment date: 25 Mar 1813 - Place: Bennington, VT - Period: 5 Yrs - Enlisted by whom: Charles Follett - Prisoner of War, disabled from wounds (no further information found).

Thomson, Abram - Private - 31st US Infantry - Age: 27 - Height: 5' 6" - Eyes: Black - Hair: Black - Complexion: Black - Born: New York, NY - Trade: Farmer - Enlistment date: 2 Nov 1814 - Place: Guilford or Brattleboro, VA - Period: War - Enlisted by whom: Jeremiah Greenleaf - Pension: Listed as Abraham Thompson on his land bounty warrant - BLW 4995-160-12 - Discharged at Woodstock, VT, on 31 Mar 1815.

Toby, James - Recruit - 26th US Infantry - Recruiting Detachment: William Bezeau - Age: 31 - Height: 5' 10 1/2" - Eyes: Black - Hair: Curly - Complexion: Brown - Born: Delaware - Trade: Farmer - Enlistment date: 19 Jan 1815 - Place: Philadelphia - Period: War - Enlisted by whom: William Bezeau - Listed on the Descriptive Roll of 1 Apr 1815; deserted on 24 Jan 1815.

Townsend, James - Private - US Light Artillery - Company: John McIntosh - Age: 20 - Height: 5' 7" - Eyes: Black - Hair: Black - Complexion: Black - Born: Newson, NY - Trade: Laborer - Enlistment date: 18 Jul 1814 - Place: Boston - Period: War - Enlisted by whom: Samuel Washburn - Discharged at Plattsburg, NY, on 31 May 1815.

Townsend, Jonathan - Laborer – U.S. Corps of Artificers - Company: Alexander Parris - Other regiment: 9th Infantry then 5th Infantry - Age: 25 - Height: 5' 6" - Born: N. Salem, Hampshire County, MA - Trade: Blacksmith - Enlistment date: 19 Feb 1813 - Period: 5 Yrs - Enlisted in the 9th Infantry, attached to the U.S. Corps of Artificers at Plattsburgh, NY, on 1 May 1814, transferred to the 5th Infantry, deserted at Detroit, MI, on 26 Jun 1816, listed as "Black" in *A List of Pensioners of the War of 1812.*

Tredwell, Cyrus - Musician - 27th US Infantry - Company: Allen Reynolds - Age: 21 - Height: 5' 9" - Eyes: Hazel - Hair: Black - Complexion: Yellow or Black - Born: Long Island, NY - Trade: Musician - Enlistment date: 16 Sep 1814 - Place: New York - Period: War - Enlisted by whom: Allen Reynolds - Discharged on 20 Jun 1815.

Trusty, Campbell - Recruit - 26th US Infantry - Recruiting Detachment: William Bezeau - Age: 23 - Height: 6' 1" - Eyes: Black - Hair: Curly - Complexion: Black - Born: Delaware - Trade: Laborer - Enlistment date: 3 Nov 1814 - Place: Philadelphia - Period: War - Enlisted by whom: William Bezeau - BLW 5296-160-12 - Listed as "Colored" in his service record; discharged at Philadelphia on 23 Mar 1815.

Turner, Caesar - Recruit - 26th US Infantry - Recruiting Detachment: William Bezeau - Age: 40 - Height: 5' 8" - Born: Pennsylvania - Enlistment date: 29 Nov 1814 - Place: Philadelphia - Enlisted by whom: William Bezeau - Listed as "Col'd" in his service record.

Valloon, Abraham - Private - 11th US Infantry - Company: William Foster - Other regiment: 6th US Infantry - Age: 24 - Height: 5' 10" - Eyes: Black - Hair: Black - Complexion: Black - Born: Lunenburg, VT - Trade: Farmer - Enlistment date: 13 May 1814 - Place: Bennington, VT - Period: 5 Yrs - Enlisted by whom: John Walker - Discharged before 30 Jun 1816.

Van Kamp, Joseph - Recruit - 26th US Infantry - Recruiting Detachment: William Bezeau - Age: 21 - Height: - Eyes: Black - Hair: Black - Complexion: Brown - Born: Pennsylvania - Trade: Laborer - Enlistment date: 25 Oct 1814 - Place: Philadelphia - Period: War - Enlisted by whom: William Bezeau - BLW 7209-160-12 - Listed as "Col'd" in his service record; discharged at Philadelphia on 20 Mar 1815.

Vineburner, Andrew (Venbunar) - Recruit - 26th US Infantry - Recruiting Detachment: William Bezeau - Age: 34 - Height: 5' 8 1/2" - Eyes: Brown - Hair: Curly - Complexion: Yellow - Born: New York - Trade: Laborer - Enlistment date: 23 Nov 1814 - Place: Philadelphia - Period: War - Enlisted by whom: William Bezeau - BLW 51294-160-12 - Listed as "Col'd" in his service record; discharged at Philadelphia on 20 Mar 1815.

Wallace, Warner - Recruit - 26th US Infantry - Recruiting Detachment: William Bezeau - Age: 19 - Height: 5' 8 1/2" - Eyes: Black - Hair: Curly - Complexion: Black - Born: New Jersey - Trade: Farmer - Enlistment date: 26 Dec 1814 - Place: Philadelphia - Period: War - Enlisted by whom: William Bezeau - Listed as "Col'd" in his service record; died in general hospital on 14 Mar 1815.

Wanton, Thomas - Private - US Light Artillery - Company: George Morris - Age: 18 - Height: 5' 6" - Eyes: Black - Hair: Black - Complexion: Black - Born: Narragansett, RI - Trade: Farmer - Enlistment date: 15 Aug 1814 - Place: Providence, RI - Period: War - Enlisted by whom: William Campbell - Discharged on 31 Mar 1815.

Warman, Thomas - Recruit - 26th US Infantry - Recruiting Detachment: William Bezeau - Age: 36 - Height: 6' - Eyes: Dark - Hair: Dark - Complexion: Brown - Born: New Jersey - Trade: Cooper - Enlistment date: 16 Jan 1815 - Place: Philadelphia - Period: War - Enlisted by whom: William Bezeau - Listed on the Descriptive Roll of 1 Apr 1815; deserted on 24 Jan 1815.

Watson, Allen - Private - 26th US Infantry - Recruiting Detachment: William Bezeau - Age: 21 - Height: 5' 2" - Eyes: Dark - Hair: Brown - Complexion: Brown - Born: Pennsylvania - Trade: Farmer - Enlistment date: 18 Jan 1815 - Place: Philadelphia - Period: War - Enlisted by whom: William Bezeau - Listed on the Descriptive Roll of 1 Apr 1815.

Weldrum, Andrew (Weldron) - Recruit - 26th US Infantry - Recruiting Detachment: William Bezeau - Age: 31 - Height: 5' 6" - Eyes: Brown - Hair: Brown - Complexion: Yellow - Born: Philadelphia - Trade: Farmer - Enlistment date: 3 Sep 1814 - Place: Philadelphia - Period: 5 Yrs - Enlisted by whom: William Bezeau - Listed as a "Negro" in his service record; discharged at Philadelphia on 13 May 1815.

Welton, Charles - Recruit - 26th US Infantry - Recruiting Detachment: William Bezeau - Age: 21 - Height: 5' 4" - Eyes: Black - Hair: Curly - Complexion: Brown - Born: Pennsylvania - Trade: Farmer - Enlistment date: 9 Jan 1815 - Place: Philadelphia - Period: War - Enlisted by whom: William Bezeau - Listed on the Descriptive Roll of 1 Apr 1815.

Welton, George - Recruit - 26th US Infantry - Recruiting Detachment: William Bezeau - Age: 27 - Height: 5' 11" - Eyes: Black - Hair: Curly - Complexion: Black - Born: Delaware - Trade: Farmer - Enlistment date: 4 Feb 1815 - Place: Philadelphia - Period: War - Enlisted by whom: William Bezeau - Listed on the Descriptive Roll of Colored Men, 1 Apr 1815.

Wendell, Joseph (Wendall) - Private - US Light Artillery - Company: John McIntosh - Age: 20 - Height: 5' 5" - Eyes: Black - Hair: Black - Complexion: Black - Born: Boston - Trade: Rope maker - Enlistment date: 15 Jul 1814 - Place: Boston - Period: War - Enlisted by whom: Samuel Washburn - BLW 11680-160-42 - Discharged at Plattsburg, NY, on 31 May 1815.

Wensell, Philip - Private - 1st US Infantry - Company: Hugh Moore - Age: 25 - Height: 5' 7" - Eyes: Hazel - Hair: Black - Complexion: Black - Born: Westmoreland County, PA - Trade: Farmer - Enlistment date: 24 Feb 1812 - Place: Greenburg, PA - Period: 5 Yrs - Enlisted by whom: McGunigle - Died at Fort Wayne, IN, on 25 Feb 1814 from dropsy.

Wharton, Murray - Recruit - 26th US Infantry - Recruiting Detachment: William Bezeau - Age: 22 - Height: 5' 8" - Eyes: Black - Hair: Curly - Complexion: Black - Born: Africa - Trade: Tanner - Enlistment date: 4 Oct 1814 - Place: Philadelphia - Period: War - Enlisted by whom: William Bezeau - Listed as "Col'd" in his service record; deserted at Lazaretto, PA, on 30 Mar 1815.

Wheelock, Ezra - Laborer – U.S. Corps of Artificers - Company: Alexander Parris - Other regiment: 4th Infantry then the 5th Infantry - Age: 25 - Height: 5' 4" - Born: Worcester, MA - Trade: Blacksmith - Enlistment date: 9 Feb 1813 - Place: War - Period: Worcester, MA - BLW 11725-160-12 - Enlisted in the 4th Infantry, on extra duty in the Quartermaster General's Department on 28 Feb 1815, transferred to the 5th Infantry, discharged at Greenbush, NY, on 1 May 1815; listed as "Black" in *A List of Pensioners of the War of 1812*.

Wilton – see George Welton

White, Charles - Recruit - 26th US Infantry - Recruiting Detachment: William Bezeau - Age: 21 - Height: 5' 5" - Eyes: Black - Hair: Curly - Complexion: Black - Born: Delaware - Trade: Laborer - Enlistment date: 4 Feb 1815 - Place: Philadelphia - Period: War - Enlisted by whom: William Bezeau - Listed on the Descriptive Roll of Colored Men, 1 Apr 1815.

White, Francis - Recruit - 26th US Infantry - Recruiting Detachment: William Bezeau - Age: 23 - Height: 5' 7" - Eyes: Black - Hair: Curly - Complexion: Yellow - Born: Delaware - Trade: Sailor - Enlistment date: 27 Nov 1814 - Place: Philadelphia - Period: War - Enlisted by whom: William Bezeau - Listed as "Col'd" in his service record; deserted on 10 Dec 1814.

White, James - Recruit - 26th US Infantry - Recruiting Detachment: William Bezeau - Age: 23 - Height: 5' 10" - Eyes: Black - Hair: Black - Complexion: Black - Born: Pennsylvania - Trade: Farmer - Enlistment date: 25 Oct 1814 - Place: Philadelphia - Period: 5 Yrs - Enlisted by whom: William Bezeau - Listed as "Col'd" in his service record; discharged at Philadelphia on 17 May 1815.

White, Thomas - Recruit - 26th US Infantry - Recruiting Detachment: William Bezeau - Age: 27 - Height: 6' - Eyes: Black - Hair: Curly - Complexion: Yellow - Born: Pennsylvania - Trade: Farmer - Enlistment date: 18 Jan 1815 - Place: Philadelphia - Period: War - Enlisted by whom: William Bezeau - Listed on the Descriptive Roll of Colored Men, 1 Apr 1815.

White, William - Recruit - 26th US Infantry - Recruiting Detachment: William Bezeau - Age: 17 -

Height: 4' 8" - Eyes: Black - Hair: Curly - Complexion: Black - Born: Maryland - Trade: Laborer - Enlistment date: 11 Oct 1814 - Place: Philadelphia - Period: War - Enlisted by whom: William Bezeau - Listed as "Colored" and "Col'd" in his service record.

Wigham, Robert - Recruit - 26th US Infantry - Recruiting Detachment: William Bezeau - Age: 28 - Height: 5' 9" - Eyes: Black - Hair: Curly - Complexion: Black - Born: Delaware - Trade: Farmer - Enlistment date: 26 Jan 1815 - Place: Philadelphia - Period: War - Enlisted by whom: William Bezeau - Listed on the Descriptive Roll of Colored Men, 1 Apr 1815.

Willett, Edward - Recruit - 26th US Infantry - Recruiting Detachment: William Bezeau - Age: 21 - Height: 5' 8 1/2" - Eyes: Black - Hair: Black - Complexion: Dark - Born: New Jersey - Trade: Farmer - Enlistment date: 13 Sep 1814 - Place: Philadelphia - Period: 5 Yrs - Enlisted by whom: William Bezeau - Listed as a "Negro" in his service record; discharged at Philadelphia on 20 May 1815.

Williams, Cato - Private - 11th US Infantry - Company: John Bliss - Age: 30 - Height: 5' 5 1/2" - Eyes: Black - Hair: Black - Complexion: Black - Born: Lanesborough, MA - Trade: Farmer - Enlistment date: 24 May 1812 - Period: 5 Yrs - Enlisted by whom: Samuel Holley - Absent with the US Navy on Lake Champlain.

Williams, Charles - Private - US Light Artillery - Company: George Morris - Age: 24 - Height: 5' 9" - Eyes: Black - Hair: Black - Complexion: Black or Dark - Born: Philadelphia - Trade: Mariner - Enlistment date: 29 Sep 1814 - Place: Boston - Period: War - Enlisted by whom: William Campbell - Discharged on 31 Mar 1815.

Williams, Henry - Private - US Light Artillery - Company: George Morris - Age: 33 - Height: 5' 5 1/2" - Eyes: Black - Hair: Black - Complexion: Black - Born: St. Croix, Danish West Indies - Trade: Laborer - Enlistment date: 3 Oct 1814 - Period: War - Enlisted by whom: William Campbell.

Williams, John - Recruit - 26th US Infantry - Recruiting Detachment: William Bezeau - Age: 20 - Height: 5' 8" - Eyes: Black - Hair: Curly - Complexion: Yellow - Born: Philadelphia - Trade: Laborer - Enlistment date: 16 Oct 1814 - Place: Philadelphia - Period: War - Enlisted by whom: William Bezeau - BLW 7211-160-12 - Listed as "Col'd" in his service record; discharged at Philadelphia discharged on 23 Mar 1815.

Williams, William - Corporal - 38th US Infantry - Company: Shepperd Leakin - Age: 22 - Height: 5' 8" - Eyes: Grey - Hair: Black - Complexion: Dark - Born: Baltimore - Trade: Laborer - Enlistment date: 5 Apr 1814 - Period: War - Enlisted by whom: John Martin - A Mulatto who also used the name "Frederick Hall."

Willis, Henry - Private - 29th US Infantry - Company: John Rochester - Age: 21 - Height: 5' 10" - Eyes: Black - Hair: Black - Complexion: Black - Born: Stockbridge, MA - Trade: Laborer - Enlistment date: 6 Jul 1814 - Place: Troy, NY - Period: 5 Yrs - Enlisted by whom: Gad. Dumbleton - Deserted at Half Moon, NY, on 25 or 26 Apr 1816.

Willis, Henry - Private - 29th US Infantry - Company: John Rochester - Other regiment: 6th US Infantry - Age: 21 - Height: 5' 10" - Eyes: Black - Hair: Black - Complexion: Black - Born: Stockbridge, MA - Trade: Laborer - Enlistment date: 6 Jul 1814 - Place: Troy, NY - Period: 5 Yrs - Enlisted by whom: Gad. Dumbleton.

Willitz – Edward Willett

Wilson, Charles - Recruit - 26th US Infantry - Recruiting Detachment: William Bezeau - Age: 30 - Height: 5' 3" - Eyes: Black - Hair: Black - Complexion: Dark - Born: Africa - Trade: Laborer - Enlistment date: 19 Oct 1814 - Place: Philadelphia - Period: War - Enlisted by whom: William Bezeau - BLW 14827-160-12 - Listed as "Col'd" in his service record; discharged at Philadelphia on 20 Mar 1815.

Wilson, Robert - Recruit - 26th US Infantry - Recruiting Detachment: William Bezeau - Age: 21 - Height: 5' 6" - Eyes: Black - Hair: Curly - Complexion: Yellow - Born: Connecticut - Trade: Wisp maker - Enlistment date: 24 Nov 1814 - Place: Philadelphia - Period: 5 Yrs - Enlisted by whom: William Bezeau - Listed as "Colored" in his service record; discharged at Philadelphia on 1 Jun 1815.

Wiman, Ebenezer - Laborer – U.S. Corps of Artificers - Company: Alexander Parris - Listed as "Black" in *A List of Pensioners of the War of 1812*.

Winn, Henry - Recruit - 26th US Infantry - Recruiting Detachment: William Bezeau - Age: 25 - Height: 5' 5" - Eyes: Black - Hair: Black - Complexion: Yellow - Born: Maryland - Trade: Farmer - Enlistment date: 9 Oct 1814 - Place: Philadelphia - Period: War - Enlisted by whom: William Bezeau - Listed as "Col'd" in his service record; discharged on 20 Mar 1815.

Winn, James - Recruit - 26th US Infantry - Recruiting Detachment: William Bezeau - Age: 22 - Height: 5' 5" - Eyes: Black - Hair: Curly - Complexion: Yellow or Black - Born: Maryland - Trade: Laborer - Enlistment date: 10 Oct 1814 - Place: Philadelphia - Period: 5 Yrs - Enlisted by whom: William Bezeau - BLW 10299-160-12 - Listed as "Col'd" in his service record; discharged at Philadelphia on 25 Mar 1815.

Winters, Abraham - Recruit - 26th US Infantry - Recruiting Detachment: William Bezeau - Age: 22 - Height: 5' 6" - Eyes: Black - Hair: Curly - Complexion: Brown - Born: Pennsylvania - Trade: Farmer - Enlistment date: 8 Jan 1815 - Place: Philadelphia - Period: War - Enlisted by whom: William Bezeau - Listed on the Descriptive Roll of Colored Men, 1 Apr 1815.

Winters, Peter - Recruit - 26th US Infantry - Recruiting Detachment: William Bezeau - Age: 26 - Height: 5' 5" - Eyes: Black - Hair: Curly - Complexion: Dark - Born: Delaware - Trade: Seaman - Enlistment date: 7 Dec 1814 - Place: Philadelphia - Period: 5 Yrs - Enlisted by whom: William Bezeau - Listed as "Colored" and as a "Negro" in his service record; discharged at Philadelphia on 1 May 1815.

Wright, Samuel W. - Recruit - 26th US Infantry - Recruiting Detachment: William Bezeau - Age: 23 - Height: 5' 6" - Eyes: Black - Hair: Curly - Complexion: Yellow - Born: Virginia - Enlistment date: 14 Jan 1815 - Place: Philadelphia - Period: War - Enlisted by whom: William Bezeau - Listed on the Descriptive Roll of Colored Men, 1 Apr 1815.

Wyman – see Ebenezer Wiman

Yalpin, Solomon - Recruit - 26th US Infantry - Recruiting Detachment: William Bezeau - Age: 25 - Height: 5' 4" - Eyes: Black - Hair: Curly - Complexion: Black - Born: Pennsylvania - Trade: Porter - Enlistment date: 6 Feb 1815 - Place: Philadelphia - Period: 5 Yrs - Enlisted by whom: William Bezeau - Listed on the Descriptive Roll of Colored Men, 1 Apr 1815.

Yanton, Smith - Recruit - 26th US Infantry - Recruiting Detachment: William Bezeau - Age: 28 - Height: 5' 8" - Eyes: Black - Hair: Curly - Complexion: Black - Born: Pennsylvania - Trade: Laborer -

Enlistment date: 6 Feb 1815 - Place: Philadelphia - Period: War - Enlisted by whom: William Bezeau - Listed on the Descriptive Roll of Colored Men, 1 Apr 1815.

York, Tobias - Recruit - 26th US Infantry - Recruiting Detachment: William Bezeau - Age: 30 - Height: 5' 10" - Eyes: Black - Hair: Black - Complexion: Black - Born: Maryland - Trade: Laborer - Enlistment date: 13 Oct 1814 - Place: Philadelphia - Period: War - Enlisted by whom: William Bezeau - Listed as "Col'd" in his service record; deserted on 11 Nov 1814.

Youell, Daniel Thomas - Private - 30th US Infantry - Company: William Miller - Age: 24 - Height: 5' 8" - Eyes: Black - Hair: Curly - Complexion: Black - Born: New York, NY - Trade: Farmer - Enlistment date: 21 Mar 1814 - Place: Burlington, VT - Period: War - Enlisted by whom: William Barney - Deserted at Plattsburg, NY, on 7 or 11 Sep 1814.

Young, Francis - Recruit - 26th US Infantry - Recruiting Detachment: William Bezeau - Age: 23 - Height: 5' 4" - Eyes: Black - Hair: Curly - Complexion: Black - Born: Pennsylvania - Trade: Brass pounder - Enlistment date: 27 Oct 1814 - Place: Philadelphia - Period: War - Enlisted by whom: William Bezeau - Listed as "Col'd" in his service record; deserted on 11 Nov 1814.

Young, Samuel - Recruit - 26th US Infantry - Recruiting Detachment: William Bezeau - Age: 20 - Height: 5' 9" - Eyes: Black - Hair: Curly - Complexion: Black - Born: Pennsylvania - Trade: Carter - Enlistment date: 28 Jan 1815 - Place: Philadelphia - Period: War - Enlisted by whom: William Bezeau - Listed on the Descriptive Roll of Colored Men, 1 Apr 1815.

Youngblood, Joseph - Private - 24th US Infantry - Company: Robert Desha - Age: 26 - Height: 5' 5 1/2" - Eyes: Black - Hair: Black - Complexion: Yellow - Born: Charleston, SC - Trade: Carpenter - Enlistment date: 5 Feb 1815 - Place: Nashville, TN - Period: War - Enlisted by whom: Lieutenant Perkins - BLW 260-320-42 - Discharged at Nashville, TN, on 26 Apr 1815.

Youngsted, Hope (Yousted) - Recruit - 26th US Infantry - Recruiting Detachment: William Bezeau - Age: 24 - Height: 5' 11" - Eyes: Black - Hair: Curly - Complexion: Black - Born: Pennsylvania - Trade: Laborer - Enlistment date: 27 Jan 1815 - Place: Philadelphia - Period: War - Enlisted by whom: William Bezeau - Pension: First land bounty was cancelled by an order of the War Department, 19 May 1820 - BLW 811-320-14 Cancelled; BLW 1037-320-14 - Listed on the Descriptive Roll of Colored Men, 1 Apr 1815.

The Militiamen

(A Black) Sam - Waiter - Brigadier General William Colfax's Brigade, New Jersey Militia.

(A Blackman) William - Servant - 5th Regiment, Maryland Militia (Lieutenant Colonel Joseph Sterett).

(Blackman) Anthony - Waiter - Major Isaac Andruss' Battalion, New Jersey Militia.

(Blackman) Peter - Servant - 52nd Regiment, Virginia Militia (Lieutenant Colonel John H. Christian).

(Blk Boy) George - Servant - 2nd Regiment, Virginia Militia (Colonel Thomas Ballowe).

(Boy) George - Servant - 9th Regiment, Virginia Militia (Lieutenant Colonel William Sharp).

(Negro) Aaron - Servant - 65th Regiment, Virginia Militia.

(Negro) Alexander - Servant - 7th Cavalry Regiment, Maryland Militia (Lieutenant Colonel John Streett).

(Negro) Alford - Servant - Lieutenant Colonel Thomas Hinds' Cavalry Battalion, Mississippi Militia.

(Negro) Anthony - Servant - 57th Regiment, Virginia Militia (Colonel Armistead J. Mason).

(Negro) Ben - Servant - 7th Cavalry Regiment, Maryland Militia (Lieutenant Colonel John Streett).

(Negro) Benjamin - Servant - Lieutenant Colonel Thomas Hinds' Cavalry Battalion, Mississippi Militia.

(Negro) Brown, Ignatius - Servant - 3rd Division, Maryland Militia (Brigadier General Samuel Smith).

(Negro) Esly - Servant - 57th Regiment, Virginia Militia (Colonel Armistead J. Mason).

(Negro) Ford, James - Servant - 1st Regiment, District of Columbia Militia.

(Negro) Frank - Waiter - 2nd Regiment, Georgia Militia (Colonel Jett Thomas).

(Negro) George - Servant - 7th Cavalry Regiment, Maryland Militia (Lieutenant Colonel John Streett).

(Negro) George - Servant - 3rd Division, Maryland Militia (Brigadier General Samuel Smith).

(Negro) Humphries - Waiter - 2nd Regiment, Georgia Militia (Colonel Jett Thomas).

(Negro) Jimmy - Sergeant - 65th Regiment, Virginia Militia.

(Negro) Manuel - Servant - 17th, 18th and 19th Consolidated Regiment, Louisiana Militia.

(Negro) Peter - Servant - 3rd Division, Maryland Militia (Brigadier General Samuel Smith).

(Negro) Peter - Servant - 1st Regiment, Virginia Militia (Lieutenant Colonel Charles Yancey).

(Negro) Phillip - Servant - 1st Regiment, Virginia Militia (Lieutenant Colonel William Trueheart).

(Negro) Sam - Waiter - 3rd Regiment, West Tennessee Militia (Colonel James Roulston).

The Militiamen

(Negro) Thomas - Servant - 49th Regiment, Maryland Militia (Lieutenant Colonel Thomas W. Veazey).

(Negro) Thomas - Servant - 3rd Division, Maryland Militia (Brigadier General Samuel Smith).

(Negro) Thomas - Servant - 40th Regiment, Maryland Militia (Lieutenant Colonel Andrew Turner).

(Negro) Thomas - Waiter - 42nd Regiment, Maryland Militia (Lieutenant Colonel William Smith).

(Negro) William - Waiter - Lieutenant Colonel David Neilson's Detachment, Mississippi Militia.

(Negro) William - Waiter - 2nd Regiment, West Tennessee Militia (Colonel John Cocke).

(Negro) William - Servant - 27th Regiment, Maryland Militia (Colonel Kennedy Long).

(Negro) Willis - Servant - Major William Woodfolk's Battalion, Tennessee Militia.

(Negro) Wilsey, Cornelius - Servant - Lieutenant Colonel Jonathan Varian's Regiment, New York Militia.

-----, Geoffry - Servant - Major General Nathaniel Watson's Division, Pennsylvania Militia - Company: Headquarter Staff - Enlistment date: 5 Sep 1814 - Negro servant to Major Christian Spayd, Assistant Adjutant General; served in the relief of Fort McHenry, MD.

-----, John - Servant - Major General Nathaniel Watson's Division, Pennsylvania Militia - Company: Headquarter Staff - Enlistment date: 28 Sep 1814 - Negro servant to Dr. Samuel Agnew, Hospital Surgeon; served in the relief of Fort McHenry, MD.

-----, Joseph - Servant - Major General Nathaniel Watson's Division, Pennsylvania Militia - Company: Headquarter Staff - Enlistment date: 3 Dec 1814 - Negro servant to Dr. Luther Reily, Hospital Mate; served in the relief of Fort McHenry, MD.

-----, Joseph - Servant - Major General Nathaniel Watson's Division, Pennsylvania Militia - Company: Headquarter Staff - Enlistment date: 1 Sep 1814 - Negro servant to Major Henry Shippen, Aide-de-camp; served in the relief of Fort McHenry, MD.

-----, Richard - Servant - Major General Nathaniel Watson's Division, Pennsylvania Militia - Company: Headquarter Staff - Enlistment date: 1 Sep 1814 - Negro servant to Major General Nathaniel Watson; served in the relief of Fort McHenry, MD.

-----, Samuel - Servant - Major General Nathaniel Watson's Division, Pennsylvania Militia - Company: Headquarter Staff - Enlistment date: 10 Sep 1814 - Negro servant to Colonel Henry Miller, Deputy Quartermaster General; served in the relief of Fort McHenry, MD.

Alexandre, Charles - Private - Major Louis D'Aquin's 2nd Battalion, Louisiana Militia.

Alexandre, Ezaine - Private - Lieutenant Colonel Michael Fortier's 1st Battalion, Louisiana Militia.

Allegre, Charles - Private - Lieutenant Colonel Michael Fortier's 1st Battalion, Louisiana Militia.

Alleque, Narcesse - Sergeant - Lieutenant Colonel Michael Fortier's 1st Battalion, Louisiana Militia.

Almajor, Joseph - Second Lieutenant - Lieutenant Colonel Michael Fortier's 1st Battalion, Louisiana Militia.

Black Regulars and Militiamen in the War of 1812

Alom, Benito - Private - Lieutenant Colonel Michael Fortier's 1st Battalion, Louisiana Militia.

Amelin, Julien - Private - Lieutenant Colonel Michael Fortier's 1st Battalion, Louisiana Militia.

Amotte, Cherubin - Private - Major Louis D'Aquin's 2nd Battalion, Louisiana Militia.

Amotte, Zami - Private - Major Louis D'Aquin's 2nd Battalion, Louisiana Militia.

Armires, Etienne - Sergeant - Lieutenant Colonel Michael Fortier's 1st Battalion, Louisiana Militia.

Asmar, Baptiste - Private - Lieutenant Colonel Michael Fortier's 1st Battalion, Louisiana Militia.

Asmard, Joisim - Sergeant - Lieutenant Colonel Michael Fortier's 1st Battalion, Louisiana Militia.

Astier, Jean Louis - Corporal - Lieutenant Colonel Michael Fortier's 1st Battalion, Louisiana Militia.

Aubrey, Marcelin - Private - Lieutenant Colonel Michael Fortier's 1st Battalion, Louisiana Militia.

Aubrey, Pierre - Private - Lieutenant Colonel Michael Fortier's 1st Battalion, Louisiana Militia.

Auguste, Jean Baptiste - Private - Major Louis D'Aquin's 2nd Battalion, Louisiana Militia.

Auguste, Moliere - Private - Lieutenant Colonel Michael Fortier's 1st Battalion, Louisiana Militia.

Auguste, Voltaire - Private - Lieutenant Colonel Michael Fortier's 1st Battalion, Louisiana Militia.

Augustin, Joseph - Private - Lieutenant Colonel Michael Fortier's 1st Battalion, Louisiana Militia.

Augustin, Pierre - Private - Major Louis D'Aquin's 2nd Battalion, Louisiana Militia.

Bachalier, Cadet - Private - Major Louis D'Aquin's 2nd Battalion, Louisiana Militia.

Bactave, Belas - Private - Major Louis D'Aquin's 2nd Battalion, Louisiana Militia.

Bactave, Bienaime - Private - Major Louis D'Aquin's 2nd Battalion, Louisiana Militia.

Badell, Pierre - Private - Lieutenant Colonel Michael Fortier's 1st Battalion, Louisiana Militia.

Badille, Jacques - Sergeant - Lieutenant Colonel Michael Fortier's 1st Battalion, Louisiana Militia.

Badille, Pierre - Private - Lieutenant Colonel Michael Fortier's 1st Battalion, Louisiana Militia.

Bague, Tedenzur - Corporal - Major Louis D'Aquin's 2nd Battalion, Louisiana Militia.

Bailly, Pierre - Private - Lieutenant Colonel Michael Fortier's 1st Battalion, Louisiana Militia.

Bailly, Pierre Fils - Private - Lieutenant Colonel Michael Fortier's 1st Battalion, Louisiana Militia.

Baptiste, Jean - Musician - Lieutenant Colonel Michael Fortier's 1st Battalion, Louisiana Militia.

Baptiste, Jean - Private - Major Louis D'Aquin's 2nd Battalion, Louisiana Militia.

The Militiamen

Baptiste, Jn. - Servant - Major Louis D'Aquin's 2nd Battalion, Louisiana Militia.

Baptiste, Jn. - Sergeant - Major Louis D'Aquin's 2nd Battalion, Louisiana Militia.

Baptiste, John - Drummer - Major Louis D'Aquin's 2nd Battalion, Louisiana Militia.

Barbe, Mathiew - Private - Lieutenant Colonel Michael Fortier's 1st Battalion, Louisiana Militia.

Barget, Louis - Private - Major Louis D'Aquin's 2nd Battalion, Louisiana Militia.

Barnabe, Jean Baptiste - Private - Lieutenant Colonel Michael Fortier's 1st Battalion, Louisiana Militia.

Barons, Etienne - Private - Lieutenant Colonel Michael Fortier's 1st Battalion, Louisiana Militia.

Barte, Pierre - Private - Lieutenant Colonel Michael Fortier's 1st Battalion, Louisiana Militia.

Bartle, Jean - Private - Lieutenant Colonel Michael Fortier's 1st Battalion, Louisiana Militia.

Bay Jupiter - Servant - 3rd Regiment, New Jersey Militia (Colonel John Frelinghuysen).

Beaudeud, Seraphin - Private - Lieutenant Colonel Michael Fortier's 1st Battalion, Louisiana Militia.

Beaulieau, Nerlin - Private - Lieutenant Colonel Michael Fortier's 1st Battalion, Louisiana Militia.

Beaulieau, Urbaim - Private - Lieutenant Colonel Michael Fortier's 1st Battalion, Louisiana Militia.

Beaulieu, Elienne - Private - Lieutenant Colonel Michael Fortier's 1st Battalion, Louisiana Militia.

Beaulieu, Gilbert - Private - Lieutenant Colonel Michael Fortier's 1st Battalion, Louisiana Militia.

Beaulieu, Jean Baptiste - Private - Lieutenant Colonel Michael Fortier's 1st Battalion, Louisiana Militia.

Beaulieu, Kuiben - Private - Lieutenant Colonel Michael Fortier's 1st Battalion, Louisiana Militia.

Beaulieu, Lendon - Private - Lieutenant Colonel Michael Fortier's 1st Battalion, Louisiana Militia.

Beaulieu, Maurice - Private - Lieutenant Colonel Michael Fortier's 1st Battalion, Louisiana Militia.

Beaulieu, Philippe - Private - Lieutenant Colonel Michael Fortier's 1st Battalion, Louisiana Militia.

Belair, Jean - Corporal - Lieutenant Colonel Michael Fortier's 1st Battalion, Louisiana Militia.

Belbadert, Celestin - Private - Major Louis D'Aquin's 2nd Battalion, Louisiana Militia.

Benoit, Baptiste - Private - Lieutenant Colonel Michael Fortier's 1st Battalion, Louisiana Militia.

Beranard, Sanon - Private - Lieutenant Colonel Michael Fortier's 1st Battalion, Louisiana Militia.

Bernard, J. N. - Private - Major Louis D'Aquin's 2nd Battalion, Louisiana Militia.

Bernard, Sanon - Private - Lieutenant Colonel Michael Fortier's 1st Battalion, Louisiana Militia.

Black Regulars and Militiamen in the War of 1812

Beroche, Elie - Musician - Lieutenant Colonel Michael Fortier's 1st Battalion, Louisiana Militia.

Birnvenn, Celestin - Private - Lieutenant Colonel Michael Fortier's 1st Battalion, Louisiana Militia.

Birnvenu, Berthelenne - Private - Lieutenant Colonel Michael Fortier's 1st Battalion, Louisiana Militia.

Birnvenu, Michel - Private - Lieutenant Colonel Michael Fortier's 1st Battalion, Louisiana Militia.

Bizot, Celestin - Musician - Lieutenant Colonel Michael Fortier's 1st Battalion, Louisiana Militia.

Blackman, John - Sergeant - Major Louis D'Aquin's 2nd Battalion, Louisiana Militia.

Blanchard, Jean - Private - Lieutenant Colonel Michael Fortier's 1st Battalion, Louisiana Militia.

Blk Man Caesar - Servant - 2nd Regiment, Virginia Militia (Colonel Thomas Ballowe).

Blonden, Valiene - Private - Lieutenant Colonel Michael Fortier's 1st Battalion, Louisiana Militia.

Bonssigneur, Jese - Private - Major Louis D'Aquin's 2nd Battalion, Louisiana Militia.

Boucherau, Justin - Private - Major Louis D'Aquin's 2nd Battalion, Louisiana Militia.

Boudeyr, Jean - Sergeant - Major Louis D'Aquin's 2nd Battalion, Louisiana Militia.

Bourgeois, Francois - Private - Lieutenant Colonel Michael Fortier's 1st Battalion, Louisiana Militia.

Braban, Laville - Private - Major Louis D'Aquin's 2nd Battalion, Louisiana Militia.

Brawdy, Aaron - Private - Tennessee Militia - Company: Joseph Rich - BLW 1969-160-55 – List as "Colored."

Breau, Marin - Private - Major Louis D'Aquin's 2nd Battalion, Louisiana Militia.

Brion, Basile - Sergeant - Lieutenant Colonel Michael Fortier's 1st Battalion, Louisiana Militia.

Brocard, Chery - Private - Major Louis D'Aquin's 2nd Battalion, Louisiana Militia.

Brule, Camille - Lieutenant - Major Louis D'Aquin's 2nd Battalion, Louisiana Militia.

Brule, Maumilion - Ensign - Lieutenant Colonel Michael Fortier's 1st Battalion, Louisiana Militia.

Buquet, Louis - Corporal - Major Louis D'Aquin's 2nd Battalion, Louisiana Militia.

Burel, Valcour - Private - Lieutenant Colonel Michael Fortier's 1st Battalion, Louisiana Militia.

Burond, Antoine - Private - Major Louis D'Aquin's 2nd Battalion, Louisiana Militia.

Burot, Francois - Private - Major Louis D'Aquin's 2nd Battalion, Louisiana Militia.

Cabaret, Jh. - Quartermaster Sergeant - Lieutenant Colonel Michael Fortier's 1st Battalion, Louisiana Militia.

The Militiamen

Cabette, Julien - Private - Major Louis D'Aquin's 2nd Battalion, Louisiana Militia.

Cachelier, Cadet - Private - Major Louis D'Aquin's 2nd Battalion, Louisiana Militia.

Camp, Bartny - Senior Musician - Lieutenant Colonel Michael Fortier's 1st Battalion, Louisiana Militia.

Camps, Joseph - Sergeant - Lieutenant Colonel Michael Fortier's 1st Battalion, Louisiana Militia.

Canelle, Pierre - Private - Lieutenant Colonel Michael Fortier's 1st Battalion, Louisiana Militia.

Capucin, Augustin - Private - Lieutenant Colonel Michael Fortier's 1st Battalion, Louisiana Militia.

Carian, A. - Second Lieutenant - Major Louis D'Aquin's 2nd Battalion, Louisiana Militia.

Carlon, Eliennee - Private - Major Louis D'Aquin's 2nd Battalion, Louisiana Militia.

Carlon, Francois - Private - Major Louis D'Aquin's 2nd Battalion, Louisiana Militia.

Carriere, Noel - First Lieutenant - Lieutenant Colonel Michael Fortier's 1st Battalion, Louisiana Militia.

Casenave, Chery - Private - Major Louis D'Aquin's 2nd Battalion, Louisiana Militia.

Casenave, Francois - Private - Major Louis D'Aquin's 2nd Battalion, Louisiana Militia.

Caynnor, Jacques - Private - Major Louis D'Aquin's 2nd Battalion, Louisiana Militia.

Chapelle, Jean Baptiste - Private - Lieutenant Colonel Michael Fortier's 1st Battalion, Louisiana Militia.

Chapron, Charles - Private - Lieutenant Colonel Michael Fortier's 1st Battalion, Louisiana Militia.

Charles, Jean - Private - Major Louis D'Aquin's 2nd Battalion, Louisiana Militia.

Charles, Manselin - Private - Lieutenant Colonel Michael Fortier's 1st Battalion, Louisiana Militia.

Charlote, S. - Musician - Lieutenant Colonel Michael Fortier's 1st Battalion, Louisiana Militia.

Chatry, Francois - Adjutant - Lieutenant Colonel Michael Fortier's 1st Battalion, Louisiana Militia.

Cherpantier, Lazarre - Private - Major Louis D'Aquin's 2nd Battalion, Louisiana Militia.

Chery, Pierre - Private - Major Louis D'Aquin's 2nd Battalion, Louisiana Militia.

Chevalle, Celestin - Private - Lieutenant Colonel Michael Fortier's 1st Battalion, Louisiana Militia.

Christoph, Sinforier - Private - Lieutenant Colonel Michael Fortier's 1st Battalion, Louisiana Militia.

Christophe, Fermins - Private - Lieutenant Colonel Michael Fortier's 1st Battalion, Louisiana Militia.

Clarisse, Pierre - Private - Major Louis D'Aquin's 2nd Battalion, Louisiana Militia.

Claveo, Valentin - Private - Lieutenant Colonel Michael Fortier's 1st Battalion, Louisiana Militia.

Black Regulars and Militiamen in the War of 1812

Coffey, Jean Baptiste - Private - Lieutenant Colonel Michael Fortier's 1st Battalion, Louisiana Militia.

Coglin, Honore - Private - Lieutenant Colonel Michael Fortier's 1st Battalion, Louisiana Militia.

Cornier, Becaud - Private - Major Louis D'Aquin's 2nd Battalion, Louisiana Militia.

Cornilis, Sonis - Lieutenant - Major Louis D'Aquin's 2nd Battalion, Louisiana Militia.

Coupelle, Joseph - Second Lieutenant - Lieutenant Colonel Michael Fortier's 1st Battalion, Louisiana Militia.

Courtois, Severe - Sergeant Major - Major Louis D'Aquin's 2nd Battalion, Louisiana Militia.

Coute, Frans - Private - Major Louis D'Aquin's 2nd Battalion, Louisiana Militia.

Couvreaus, Tervallon - Private - Major Louis D'Aquin's 2nd Battalion, Louisiana Militia.

Crepun, Thomas - Musician - Lieutenant Colonel Michael Fortier's 1st Battalion, Louisiana Militia.

Cubidon, Vincent - Private - Lieutenant Colonel Michael Fortier's 1st Battalion, Louisiana Militia.

Cuerael, Louis - Private - Lieutenant Colonel Michael Fortier's 1st Battalion, Louisiana Militia.

Curail, Lewis - Private - Lieutenant Colonel Michael Fortier's 1st Battalion, Louisiana Militia.

Cureuil, Louis - Private - Lieutenant Colonel Michael Fortier's 1st Battalion, Louisiana Militia.

Dablon, Honore - Private - Lieutenant Colonel Michael Fortier's 1st Battalion, Louisiana Militia.

Daqwin, Melvin - Second Lieutenant - Major Louis D'Aquin's 2nd Battalion, Louisiana Militia.

Darby, William - Private - Lieutenant Colonel Michael Fortier's 1st Battalion, Louisiana Militia.

Dardenel, Ponpon - Private - Major Louis D'Aquin's 2nd Battalion, Louisiana Militia.

Dauard, Vulmond - Private - Lieutenant Colonel Michael Fortier's 1st Battalion, Louisiana Militia.

Dauncey, Lous - Private - Lieutenant Colonel Michael Fortier's 1st Battalion, Louisiana Militia.

Davias, John - Sergeant - Major Louis D'Aquin's 2nd Battalion, Louisiana Militia.

Degae, Jean B. - Private - Lieutenant Colonel Michael Fortier's 1st Battalion, Louisiana Militia.

Degue, Jnobt - Private - Lieutenant Colonel Michael Fortier's 1st Battalion, Louisiana Militia.

Del Terriblo, Juan - Private - Lieutenant Colonel Michael Fortier's 1st Battalion, Louisiana Militia.

Deland, Louis - Second Lieutenant - Lieutenant Colonel Michael Fortier's 1st Battalion, Louisiana Militia.

Deland, Molbere - Second Lieutenant - Lieutenant Colonel Michael Fortier's 1st Battalion, Louisiana Militia.

The Militiamen

Deland, Zenon - Private - Lieutenant Colonel Michael Fortier's 1st Battalion, Louisiana Militia.

Delille, Felix - Private - Lieutenant Colonel Michael Fortier's 1st Battalion, Louisiana Militia.

Demazelliere, Basile - Captain - Lieutenant Colonel Michael Fortier's 1st Battalion, Louisiana Militia.

Demouille, Yacinte - Private - Lieutenant Colonel Michael Fortier's 1st Battalion, Louisiana Militia.

Demozellier, Baltazar - First Lieutenant - Lieutenant Colonel Michael Fortier's 1st Battalion, Louisiana Militia.

Denneville, Celestin - Private - Lieutenant Colonel Michael Fortier's 1st Battalion, Louisiana Militia.

Dennis, William - Black waiter - 1st Division, New York Militia (Brigadier General Ebenezer Stevens).

Derneville, Theophile - Private - Lieutenant Colonel Michael Fortier's 1st Battalion, Louisiana Militia.

Deseuirs, Peirre - Sergeant - Lieutenant Colonel Michael Fortier's 1st Battalion, Louisiana Militia.

Deurror, Jn Marie - Sergeant - Major Louis D'Aquin's 2nd Battalion, Louisiana Militia.

Diez, Antoine - Captain - Lieutenant Colonel Michael Fortier's 1st Battalion, Louisiana Militia.

Diez, Francis - Sergeant - Lieutenant Colonel Michael Fortier's 1st Battalion, Louisiana Militia.

Dodard, Valmons - Private - Lieutenant Colonel Michael Fortier's 1st Battalion, Louisiana Militia.

Dodard, Velmont - Private - Major Louis D'Aquin's 2nd Battalion, Louisiana Militia.

Dolliole, J. - Orderly Sergeant - Lieutenant Colonel Michael Fortier's 1st Battalion, Louisiana Militia.

Dolliole, Jean Louis - Private - Lieutenant Colonel Michael Fortier's 1st Battalion, Louisiana Militia.

Dolliole, Pierre - Private - Lieutenant Colonel Michael Fortier's 1st Battalion, Louisiana Militia.

Dominique, Zenon - Private - Lieutenant Colonel Michael Fortier's 1st Battalion, Louisiana Militia.

Dorville, Narcesse - Private - Lieutenant Colonel Michael Fortier's 1st Battalion, Louisiana Militia.

Dorville, Therdone - Private - Lieutenant Colonel Michael Fortier's 1st Battalion, Louisiana Militia.

Dreux, Severin - Servant - Lieutenant Colonel Michael Fortier's 1st Battalion, Louisiana Militia.

Duconge, Chewbin - Sergeant - Major Louis D'Aquin's 2nd Battalion, Louisiana Militia.

Duconge, Frederick - Private - Major Louis D'Aquin's 2nd Battalion, Louisiana Militia.

Duconge, Pierre - Private - Major Louis D'Aquin's 2nd Battalion, Louisiana Militia.

Dufossar, Cyprien - Private - Lieutenant Colonel Michael Fortier's 1st Battalion, Louisiana Militia.

Dufresne, Lowis - Private - Major Louis D'Aquin's 2nd Battalion, Louisiana Militia.

Black Regulars and Militiamen in the War of 1812

Dugon, Levi - Private - Major Louis D'Aquin's 2nd Battalion, Louisiana Militia.

Dumoulle, Bernard - Sergeant - Lieutenant Colonel Michael Fortier's 1st Battalion, Louisiana Militia.

Dupard, Celestin - Sergeant - Lieutenant Colonel Michael Fortier's 1st Battalion, Louisiana Militia.

Dupard, Charles - Sergeant - Lieutenant Colonel Michael Fortier's 1st Battalion, Louisiana Militia.

Dupard, Hilaire - Sergeant - Lieutenant Colonel Michael Fortier's 1st Battalion, Louisiana Militia.

Dupare, August - Private - Lieutenant Colonel Michael Fortier's 1st Battalion, Louisiana Militia.

Dupare, Hilaire - Sergeant - Lieutenant Colonel Michael Fortier's 1st Battalion, Louisiana Militia.

Dupare, Pierre - Sergeant - Lieutenant Colonel Michael Fortier's 1st Battalion, Louisiana Militia.

Dupart, August - Private - Lieutenant Colonel Michael Fortier's 1st Battalion, Louisiana Militia.

Duplaissy, Joseph - Sergeant - Lieutenant Colonel Michael Fortier's 1st Battalion, Louisiana Militia.

Dupont, Preire - Servant - Lieutenant Colonel Michael Fortier's 1st Battalion, Louisiana Militia.

Dupre, Les - Private - Lieutenant Colonel Michael Fortier's 1st Battalion, Louisiana Militia.

Dupres, Jacques - Private - Lieutenant Colonel Michael Fortier's 1st Battalion, Louisiana Militia.

Dupres, Peter - Private - Major Louis D'Aquin's 2nd Battalion, Louisiana Militia.

Dupuis, Edmond - Corporal - Lieutenant Colonel Michael Fortier's 1st Battalion, Louisiana Militia.

Durand, Charles - Private - Lieutenant Colonel Michael Fortier's 1st Battalion, Louisiana Militia.

Durand, Pre - Private - Major Louis D'Aquin's 2nd Battalion, Louisiana Militia.

Duriaux, Prerre - Private - Lieutenant Colonel Michael Fortier's 1st Battalion, Louisiana Militia.

Dusson, R. - Corporal - Major Louis D'Aquin's 2nd Battalion, Louisiana Militia.

Duval, Francois - Private - Lieutenant Colonel Michael Fortier's 1st Battalion, Louisiana Militia.

Duverne, Francois - First Lieutenant - Lieutenant Colonel Michael Fortier's 1st Battalion, Louisiana Militia.

Echo, Jean Baptiste - Private - Lieutenant Colonel Michael Fortier's 1st Battalion, Louisiana Militia.

Edonary, Baptiste - Corporal - Major Louis D'Aquin's 2nd Battalion, Louisiana Militia.

Embree, Richard - Private - Mississippi Territorial Militia - Company: Thomas Phillips - Pension: SO-32554; served as a private in Captain Thomas Phillips' Company, Alabama Militia - Colored; served as a substitute for his master, Jonathan Embree.

Erven, Michelle - Private - Major Louis D'Aquin's 2nd Battalion, Louisiana Militia.

The Militiamen

Escalavon, Andore - Private - Lieutenant Colonel Michael Fortier's 1st Battalion, Louisiana Militia.

Escoh, Antoine - Corporal - Lieutenant Colonel Michael Fortier's 1st Battalion, Louisiana Militia.

Escot, Louis - Private - Lieutenant Colonel Michael Fortier's 1st Battalion, Louisiana Militia.

Etienne, Hiacinth - Private - Lieutenant Colonel Michael Fortier's 1st Battalion, Louisiana Militia.

Fauchez, Cadet - Private - Major Louis D'Aquin's 2nd Battalion, Louisiana Militia.

Favre, Lindon - Private - Lieutenant Colonel Michael Fortier's 1st Battalion, Louisiana Militia.

Favres, Lindone - Private - Lieutenant Colonel Michael Fortier's 1st Battalion, Louisiana Militia.

Ferrand, Louis Fils - Sergeant Major - Major Louis D'Aquin's 2nd Battalion, Louisiana Militia.

Fletcher, Henry - Corporal - Lieutenant Colonel Michael Fortier's 1st Battalion, Louisiana Militia.

Fondal, J. L. - Private - Lieutenant Colonel Michael Fortier's 1st Battalion, Louisiana Militia.

Fontin, Jean - Private - Major Louis D'Aquin's 2nd Battalion, Louisiana Militia.

Ford, Francois - Private - Lieutenant Colonel Michael Fortier's 1st Battalion, Louisiana Militia.

Ford, St Dusuare - Corporal - Lieutenant Colonel Michael Fortier's 1st Battalion, Louisiana Militia.

Forstall, Louis - Private - Lieutenant Colonel Michael Fortier's 1st Battalion, Louisiana Militia.

Fortier, Honore - Private - Lieutenant Colonel Michael Fortier's 1st Battalion, Louisiana Militia.

Fortier, Honore - Corporal - Lieutenant Colonel Michael Fortier's 1st Battalion, Louisiana Militia.

Fortier, Norbert - Private - Lieutenant Colonel Michael Fortier's 1st Battalion, Louisiana Militia.

Fortin, Fortune - Private - Major Louis D'Aquin's 2nd Battalion, Louisiana Militia.

Foucher, Jean - Private - Lieutenant Colonel Michael Fortier's 1st Battalion, Louisiana Militia.

Foucher, Joseph - First Lieutenant - Lieutenant Colonel Michael Fortier's 1st Battalion, Louisiana Militia.

Foucher, Patrice - Private - Lieutenant Colonel Michael Fortier's 1st Battalion, Louisiana Militia.

Foucher, Valcour - Private - Lieutenant Colonel Michael Fortier's 1st Battalion, Louisiana Militia.

Francois, Jn - Servant - Lieutenant Colonel Michael Fortier's 1st Battalion, Louisiana Militia.

Francois, Noel - Private - Lieutenant Colonel Michael Fortier's 1st Battalion, Louisiana Militia.

Francois, Ulsaire - Private - Lieutenant Colonel Michael Fortier's 1st Battalion, Louisiana Militia.

Frechinette, Honore - Private - Lieutenant Colonel Michael Fortier's 1st Battalion, Louisiana Militia.

Black Regulars and Militiamen in the War of 1812

Frick, Gh. - Private - Lieutenant Colonel Michael Fortier's 1st Battalion, Louisiana Militia.

Frontin, Jean - Private - Major Louis D'Aquin's 2nd Battalion, Louisiana Militia.

Gabrielle, Charles - Private - Lieutenant Colonel Michael Fortier's 1st Battalion, Louisiana Militia.

Gaideon, Piere - Private - Major Louis D'Aquin's 2nd Battalion, Louisiana Militia.

Gaillard, Raymond - Musician - Lieutenant Colonel Michael Fortier's 1st Battalion, Louisiana Militia.

Gallaud, Louis - First Lieutenant - Lieutenant Colonel Michael Fortier's 1st Battalion, Louisiana Militia.

Gallaud, Maximilion - Private - Lieutenant Colonel Michael Fortier's 1st Battalion, Louisiana Militia.

Gallaud, Noel - Private - Lieutenant Colonel Michael Fortier's 1st Battalion, Louisiana Militia.

Garau, Pierre - Private - Lieutenant Colonel Michael Fortier's 1st Battalion, Louisiana Militia.

Garcelle, Thomas - Private - Lieutenant Colonel Michael Fortier's 1st Battalion, Louisiana Militia.

Garcia, Manuel - Surgeon - Major Louis D'Aquin's 2nd Battalion, Louisiana Militia.

Garcie, Joseph - Private - Major Louis D'Aquin's 2nd Battalion, Louisiana Militia.

Garcille, Baptiste - Private - Lieutenant Colonel Michael Fortier's 1st Battalion, Louisiana Militia.

Garcille, Thomas - Private - Lieutenant Colonel Michael Fortier's 1st Battalion, Louisiana Militia.

Garcis, Pierre - Private - Lieutenant Colonel Michael Fortier's 1st Battalion, Louisiana Militia.

Garecile, Bb. - Private - Lieutenant Colonel Michael Fortier's 1st Battalion, Louisiana Militia.

Garrick, J. H. - Private - Lieutenant Colonel Michael Fortier's 1st Battalion, Louisiana Militia.

Garrigue, Antoine - Private - Lieutenant Colonel Michael Fortier's 1st Battalion, Louisiana Militia.

Garsille, Baptiste - Private - Lieutenant Colonel Michael Fortier's 1st Battalion, Louisiana Militia.

Garsille, Thomas - Private - Lieutenant Colonel Michael Fortier's 1st Battalion, Louisiana Militia.

Gastuque, Celicoar - Private - Major Louis D'Aquin's 2nd Battalion, Louisiana Militia.

Gatreau, Edward - Private - Major Louis D'Aquin's 2nd Battalion, Louisiana Militia.

Gautan, Augustin - Private - Major Louis D'Aquin's 2nd Battalion, Louisiana Militia.

Gautier, Richond - Private - Major Louis D'Aquin's 2nd Battalion, Louisiana Militia.

Genesnon, Ursin - Private - Lieutenant Colonel Michael Fortier's 1st Battalion, Louisiana Militia.

Gentilly, Sifroix - Private - Lieutenant Colonel Michael Fortier's 1st Battalion, Louisiana Militia.

The Militiamen

Gilara, Pierre - Corporal - Lieutenant Colonel Michael Fortier's 1st Battalion, Louisiana Militia.

Gillon, Boisbelle - Adjutant - Captain - Major Louis D'Aquin's 2nd Battalion, Louisiana Militia.

Girard, Jean - Private - Lieutenant Colonel Michael Fortier's 1st Battalion, Louisiana Militia.

Girard, John - Private - Lieutenant Colonel Michael Fortier's 1st Battalion, Louisiana Militia.

Giraudau, Louis - Private - Lieutenant Colonel Michael Fortier's 1st Battalion, Louisiana Militia.

Goastere, Erasme - Private - Lieutenant Colonel Michael Fortier's 1st Battalion, Louisiana Militia.

Gramond, Cadet - Private - Major Louis D'Aquin's 2nd Battalion, Louisiana Militia.

Gramond, Etienne - Private - Major Louis D'Aquin's 2nd Battalion, Louisiana Militia.

Gray, Spencer - Black waiter - 1st Division, New York Militia (Brigadier General Ebenezer Stevens).

Guenon, Urcins - Private - Lieutenant Colonel Michael Fortier's 1st Battalion, Louisiana Militia.

Guest, Henry - Black waiter - 1st Division, New York Militia (Brigadier General Ebenezer Stevens).

Guetraut, Cherubin - Private - Major Louis D'Aquin's 2nd Battalion, Louisiana Militia.

Guienee, Cadet - Private - Major Louis D'Aquin's 2nd Battalion, Louisiana Militia.

Guienette, Etienne - Private - Major Louis D'Aquin's 2nd Battalion, Louisiana Militia.

Guillaumett, J. - Private - Major Louis D'Aquin's 2nd Battalion, Louisiana Militia.

Guillot, Marcelin - Captain - Major Louis D'Aquin's 2nd Battalion, Louisiana Militia.

Gullaumes, Joseph - Private - Lieutenant Colonel Michael Fortier's 1st Battalion, Louisiana Militia.

Gullaurre, Joseph - Private - Lieutenant Colonel Michael Fortier's 1st Battalion, Louisiana Militia.

Gustave, Barthlomi - Servant - Major Louis D'Aquin's 2nd Battalion, Louisiana Militia.

Handry, Alexcis - Private - Lieutenant Colonel Michael Fortier's 1st Battalion, Louisiana Militia.

Hardy, Francs - Private - Major Louis D'Aquin's 2nd Battalion, Louisiana Militia.

Hardy, Jacques - Private - Lieutenant Colonel Michael Fortier's 1st Battalion, Louisiana Militia.

Harrington, John - Black waiter - 1st Division, New York Militia (Brigadier General Ebenezer Stevens).

Haszeur, Ls - Senior Musician - Lieutenant Colonel Michael Fortier's 1st Battalion, Louisiana Militia.

Henry Cold Lee - Waiter - Major Abraham Stevens' Battalion, New York Militia.

Henry, Chery - Corporal - Major Louis D'Aquin's 2nd Battalion, Louisiana Militia.

Black Regulars and Militiamen in the War of 1812

Henry, Guillaume - Private - Major Louis D'Aquin's 2nd Battalion, Louisiana Militia.

Henry, Joseph - Private - Lieutenant Colonel Michael Fortier's 1st Battalion, Louisiana Militia.

Henry, Louis - Private - Major Louis D'Aquin's 2nd Battalion, Louisiana Militia.

Hewn, Chery - Corporal - Major Louis D'Aquin's 2nd Battalion, Louisiana Militia.

Hibard, Jean - Private - Major Louis D'Aquin's 2nd Battalion, Louisiana Militia.

Hicarl, Joseph - Private - Lieutenant Colonel Michael Fortier's 1st Battalion, Louisiana Militia.

Holognier, Ls. - Private - Lieutenant Colonel Michael Fortier's 1st Battalion, Louisiana Militia.

Honore, Isidone - Second Lieutenant - Lieutenant Colonel Michael Fortier's 1st Battalion, Louisiana Militia.

Honore, Pierre - Private - Lieutenant Colonel Michael Fortier's 1st Battalion, Louisiana Militia.

Honore, Rene - Private - Lieutenant Colonel Michael Fortier's 1st Battalion, Louisiana Militia.

Hubert, Cyprien - Private - Lieutenant Colonel Michael Fortier's 1st Battalion, Louisiana Militia.

Jacques, Charles - Private - Lieutenant Colonel Michael Fortier's 1st Battalion, Louisiana Militia.

Jaideon, Pierre - Private - Major Louis D'Aquin's 2nd Battalion, Louisiana Militia.

Jalabert, Cadet - Corporal - Major Louis D'Aquin's 2nd Battalion, Louisiana Militia.

Jalim, Julien - Private - Lieutenant Colonel Michael Fortier's 1st Battalion, Louisiana Militia.

Jannol, Etienne - Private - Lieutenant Colonel Michael Fortier's 1st Battalion, Louisiana Militia.

Janol, Etienne - Private - Lieutenant Colonel Michael Fortier's 1st Battalion, Louisiana Militia.

Janol, Gabriel - Private - Lieutenant Colonel Michael Fortier's 1st Battalion, Louisiana Militia.

Janseme, Augustin - Private - Lieutenant Colonel Michael Fortier's 1st Battalion, Louisiana Militia.

Jarmin, Benjamin - Surgeon's Aid - Major Louis D'Aquin's 2nd Battalion, Louisiana Militia.

Jason, Gabriel - Private - Lieutenant Colonel Michael Fortier's 1st Battalion, Louisiana Militia.

Jean, Honore - Private - Lieutenant Colonel Michael Fortier's 1st Battalion, Louisiana Militia.

Jean, Louis - Corporal - Lieutenant Colonel Michael Fortier's 1st Battalion, Louisiana Militia.

Jean, Louis - Servant - Lieutenant Colonel Michael Fortier's 1st Battalion, Louisiana Militia.

Jeantilly, Sifrois - Private - Lieutenant Colonel Michael Fortier's 1st Battalion, Louisiana Militia.

Jercer, Jean Baptiste - Private - Major Louis D'Aquin's 2nd Battalion, Louisiana Militia.

The Militiamen

Jirard, Jean - Private - Lieutenant Colonel Michael Fortier's 1st Battalion, Louisiana Militia.

Joly, J. - Lieutenant - Major Louis D'Aquin's 2nd Battalion, Louisiana Militia.

Joseph, Bazille - Private - Lieutenant Colonel Michael Fortier's 1st Battalion, Louisiana Militia.

Joseph, Jean - Private - Major Louis D'Aquin's 2nd Battalion, Louisiana Militia.

Jourdan, Celestin - Private - Lieutenant Colonel Michael Fortier's 1st Battalion, Louisiana Militia.

Jourdan, Noel - Second Lieutenant - Lieutenant Colonel Michael Fortier's 1st Battalion, Louisiana Militia.

Journin, Joseph - Private - Major Louis D'Aquin's 2nd Battalion, Louisiana Militia.

Juing, Raphael - Corporal - Lieutenant Colonel Michael Fortier's 1st Battalion, Louisiana Militia.

King, Robert - Colored waiter - 1st Regiment, New York Militia (Lieutenant Colonel Daniel Dodge).

Labor, Francois - Private - Lieutenant Colonel Michael Fortier's 1st Battalion, Louisiana Militia.

Laby, Louis - Servant - Lieutenant Colonel Michael Fortier's 1st Battalion, Louisiana Militia.

Lachaise, Baptiste - Private - Lieutenant Colonel Michael Fortier's 1st Battalion, Louisiana Militia.

Lana, Vital - Private - Lieutenant Colonel Michael Fortier's 1st Battalion, Louisiana Militia.

Langlois, Virgile - Private - Lieutenant Colonel Michael Fortier's 1st Battalion, Louisiana Militia.

Lanna, Vital - Private - Lieutenant Colonel Michael Fortier's 1st Battalion, Louisiana Militia.

Laporte, Edmond - Private - Lieutenant Colonel Michael Fortier's 1st Battalion, Louisiana Militia.

Laporte, Rodenai - Private - Major Louis D'Aquin's 2nd Battalion, Louisiana Militia.

Lapusse, Pierre - Drummer - Major Louis D'Aquin's 2nd Battalion, Louisiana Militia.

Laquinte, Garcon - Private - Major Louis D'Aquin's 2nd Battalion, Louisiana Militia.

Larieu, Jean - Private - Lieutenant Colonel Michael Fortier's 1st Battalion, Louisiana Militia.

Larieux, Etienne - Musician - Lieutenant Colonel Michael Fortier's 1st Battalion, Louisiana Militia.

Lasour, Jacgues - Private - Lieutenant Colonel Michael Fortier's 1st Battalion, Louisiana Militia.

Latoure, Jacques - Private - Lieutenant Colonel Michael Fortier's 1st Battalion, Louisiana Militia.

Laurent, Louis - Private - Major Louis D'Aquin's 2nd Battalion, Louisiana Militia.

Lausent, Louis - Private - Major Louis D'Aquin's 2nd Battalion, Louisiana Militia.

Lavaux, Narcisse - Private - Lieutenant Colonel Michael Fortier's 1st Battalion, Louisiana Militia.

Black Regulars and Militiamen in the War of 1812

Lavigne, Francois - Private - Major Louis D'Aquin's 2nd Battalion, Louisiana Militia.

Lavigne, Joseph - Private - Lieutenant Colonel Michael Fortier's 1st Battalion, Louisiana Militia.

Lavigne, Pierre - Private - Major Louis D'Aquin's 2nd Battalion, Louisiana Militia.

Le Pott, Bellonnie - Private - Major Louis D'Aquin's 2nd Battalion, Louisiana Militia.

Leclaire, Petion - Private - Major Louis D'Aquin's 2nd Battalion, Louisiana Militia.

Leclerc, Louis - Private - Major Louis D'Aquin's 2nd Battalion, Louisiana Militia.

Leclere, Joseph - Musician - Colored Battalion, Louisiana Militia - Pension: Wife Elizabeth, WO-40213; served in the drum corps of the Colored Battalion, Louisiana Militia.

Lecompte, Auguste - Drummer - Major Louis D'Aquin's 2nd Battalion, Louisiana Militia.

Leduf, Jacques - Private - Lieutenant Colonel Michael Fortier's 1st Battalion, Louisiana Militia.

Leger, Fontange - Corporal - Major Louis D'Aquin's 2nd Battalion, Louisiana Militia.

Legre, Charles A. - Private - Lieutenant Colonel Michael Fortier's 1st Battalion, Louisiana Militia.

Legros, Germain - Private - Major Louis D'Aquin's 2nd Battalion, Louisiana Militia.

Lemaire, Moliere - Quartermaster Sergeant - Lieutenant Colonel Michael Fortier's 1st Battalion, Louisiana Militia.

Lemaire, Villeneuve - Private - Lieutenant Colonel Michael Fortier's 1st Battalion, Louisiana Militia.

Lembert, Zadique - Private - Major Louis D'Aquin's 2nd Battalion, Louisiana Militia.

Lesian, Poinci - Private - Major Louis D'Aquin's 2nd Battalion, Louisiana Militia.

Lesiau, Francois - Corporal - Major Louis D'Aquin's 2nd Battalion, Louisiana Militia.

Leveque, Jacques - Corporal - Lieutenant Colonel Michael Fortier's 1st Battalion, Louisiana Militia.

Lewis, Jacob - Drummer - Virginia Militia - Company: J. W. Beagles - Pension: SO-29670 Rejected; served as a drummer in Captains J. W. Beagles', John Linton's and J. W. Bayless' Companies, Virginia Militia – List as "Col'd."

Lindor, Pierre - Private - Major Louis D'Aquin's 2nd Battalion, Louisiana Militia.

Liotean, Ferdinand - Captain - Lieutenant Colonel Michael Fortier's 1st Battalion, Louisiana Militia.

Lolognier, L. - Private - Lieutenant Colonel Michael Fortier's 1st Battalion, Louisiana Militia.

Louis, Honore - Sergeant - Lieutenant Colonel Michael Fortier's 1st Battalion, Louisiana Militia.

Louis, Jn. - Servant - Major Louis D'Aquin's 2nd Battalion, Louisiana Militia.

The Militiamen

Louis, Joseph - Corporal - Lieutenant Colonel Michael Fortier's 1st Battalion, Louisiana Militia.

Louis, Pierre - Private - Major Louis D'Aquin's 2nd Battalion, Louisiana Militia.

Luto, Duconge - Private - Major Louis D'Aquin's 2nd Battalion, Louisiana Militia.

MacArty, Baptisse - Private - Lieutenant Colonel Michael Fortier's 1st Battalion, Louisiana Militia.

MacArty, Barthy - Private - Major Louis D'Aquin's 2nd Battalion, Louisiana Militia.

MacArty, Francois - Private - Lieutenant Colonel Michael Fortier's 1st Battalion, Louisiana Militia.

Magnant, Louis - Private - Major Louis D'Aquin's 2nd Battalion, Louisiana Militia.

Malas, Edouand - Private - Major Louis D'Aquin's 2nd Battalion, Louisiana Militia.

Mandeville, Vincent - Private - Lieutenant Colonel Michael Fortier's 1st Battalion, Louisiana Militia.

Manija, Silvin - Sergeant - Major Louis D'Aquin's 2nd Battalion, Louisiana Militia.

Marchant, Hugue - Private - Major Louis D'Aquin's 2nd Battalion, Louisiana Militia.

Marie, Gabriel Jean - Private - Lieutenant Colonel Michael Fortier's 1st Battalion, Louisiana Militia.

Marie, J. - Private - Major Louis D'Aquin's 2nd Battalion, Louisiana Militia.

Marie, Joseph - Private - Major Louis D'Aquin's 2nd Battalion, Louisiana Militia.

Marigny, Celestin - Sergeant - Lieutenant Colonel Michael Fortier's 1st Battalion, Louisiana Militia.

Marin, Joseph - Private - Major Louis D'Aquin's 2nd Battalion, Louisiana Militia.

Marly, Devince - Sergeant - Lieutenant Colonel Michael Fortier's 1st Battalion, Louisiana Militia.

Marly, Jean Baptiste - Private - Lieutenant Colonel Michael Fortier's 1st Battalion, Louisiana Militia.

Marly, Pierre - Private - Lieutenant Colonel Michael Fortier's 1st Battalion, Louisiana Militia.

Marrioux, Pre Charles - Lieutenant - Major Louis D'Aquin's 2nd Battalion, Louisiana Militia.

Martin, Bazile - Private - Major Louis D'Aquin's 2nd Battalion, Louisiana Militia.

Martin, J. H. - Sergeant - Lieutenant Colonel Michael Fortier's 1st Battalion, Louisiana Militia.

Mater, Louis - Private - Lieutenant Colonel Michael Fortier's 1st Battalion, Louisiana Militia.

Mather, Jean Baptiste - Corporal - Lieutenant Colonel Michael Fortier's 1st Battalion, Louisiana Militia.

Mathieu, J. - Private - Major Louis D'Aquin's 2nd Battalion, Louisiana Militia.

Matthieu, Innocent - Private - Lieutenant Colonel Michael Fortier's 1st Battalion, Louisiana Militia.

Black Regulars and Militiamen in the War of 1812

Mauraux, Manuel - Private - Lieutenant Colonel Michael Fortier's 1st Battalion, Louisiana Militia.

McCarty, Baptiste - Private - Lieutenant Colonel Michael Fortier's 1st Battalion, Louisiana Militia.

Medecingue, Jh. - Private - Lieutenant Colonel Michael Fortier's 1st Battalion, Louisiana Militia.

Medecinque, Henry - Private - Lieutenant Colonel Michael Fortier's 1st Battalion, Louisiana Militia.

Medsingue, Jeane B. - Private - Lieutenant Colonel Michael Fortier's 1st Battalion, Louisiana Militia.

Meilleur, Souis - Private - Lieutenant Colonel Michael Fortier's 1st Battalion, Louisiana Militia.

Melanie, Sanon - Private - Lieutenant Colonel Michael Fortier's 1st Battalion, Louisiana Militia.

Mello, Jh. - Private - Lieutenant Colonel Michael Fortier's 1st Battalion, Louisiana Militia.

Mello, Pierre - Corporal - Lieutenant Colonel Michael Fortier's 1st Battalion, Louisiana Militia.

Melon, Celestin - Private - Lieutenant Colonel Michael Fortier's 1st Battalion, Louisiana Militia.

Menard, Lyon - Corporal - Major Louis D'Aquin's 2nd Battalion, Louisiana Militia.

Michel, Similien - Private - Lieutenant Colonel Michael Fortier's 1st Battalion, Louisiana Militia.

Michine, Peirre - Private - Major Louis D'Aquin's 2nd Battalion, Louisiana Militia.

Michne, Jn. - Private - Major Louis D'Aquin's 2nd Battalion, Louisiana Militia.

Micline, Pierre - Private - Major Louis D'Aquin's 2nd Battalion, Louisiana Militia.

Milon, Celestin - Private - Lieutenant Colonel Michael Fortier's 1st Battalion, Louisiana Militia.

Minville, Pierre - Private - Major Louis D'Aquin's 2nd Battalion, Louisiana Militia.

Miranda, Isaac - Black waiter - 1st Division, New York Militia (Brigadier General Ebenezer Stevens).

Mondesire, Philis - Private - Major Louis D'Aquin's 2nd Battalion, Louisiana Militia.

Monferrand, Julien - Private - Lieutenant Colonel Michael Fortier's 1st Battalion, Louisiana Militia.

Monsignac, Louis - Private - Major Louis D'Aquin's 2nd Battalion, Louisiana Militia.

Montegut, Augusto - Private - Major Louis D'Aquin's 2nd Battalion, Louisiana Militia.

Montewil, Desin - Private - Major Louis D'Aquin's 2nd Battalion, Louisiana Militia.

Montreuil, Subin - Private - Lieutenant Colonel Michael Fortier's 1st Battalion, Louisiana Militia.

Moreau, George - Private - Lieutenant Colonel Michael Fortier's 1st Battalion, Louisiana Militia.

Moreau, Louis - Private - Major Louis D'Aquin's 2nd Battalion, Louisiana Militia.

The Militiamen

Moreau, Manuel - Private - Lieutenant Colonel Michael Fortier's 1st Battalion, Louisiana Militia.

Morein, Louis - Private - Major Louis D'Aquin's 2nd Battalion, Louisiana Militia.

Morin, Amant - Private - Major Louis D'Aquin's 2nd Battalion, Louisiana Militia.

Moro, George - Private - Lieutenant Colonel Michael Fortier's 1st Battalion, Louisiana Militia.

Morrison, John - Louisiana Militia - Company: Miller - Pension: SO-30175; served in Capt. Miller's Company, Louisiana Militia – List as "Colored."

Mory, Gabrielle Jean - Private - Lieutenant Colonel Michael Fortier's 1st Battalion, Louisiana Militia.

Narcisse, Pierre - Private - Lieutenant Colonel Michael Fortier's 1st Battalion, Louisiana Militia.

Negro Brooks, John - Servant - 42nd Regiment, Maryland Militia (Lieutenant Colonel William Smith).

Negro Conner, Richard - Servant - 30th Regiment, Maryland Militia (Fowler's).

Negro Hamilton - Captain's servant - 6th Regiment, Maryland Militia (Lieutenant Colonel William McDonald).

Negro Leith - Servant - 27th Regiment, Maryland Militia (Colonel Kennedy Long).

Negro Matthew - Waiter - 2nd Regiment, West Tennessee Militia (Colonel John Cocke).

Negro Moody, John - Waiter - 51st Regiment, Maryland Militia (Lieutenant Colonel Henry Amey).

Negro Andrew - Sergeant - Captain David C. Wilson's Artillery Company, Delaware Militia.

Negro Bazil - Waiter - 1st Regiment, District of Columbia Militia.

Negro Dasseng - Servant - 17th, 18th and 19th Consolidated Regiment, Louisiana Militia.

Negro David - Waiter - 2nd Regiment, West Tennessee Militia (Colonel John Cocke).

Negro David - Servant - 5th Regiment, Virginia Militia (Lieutenant Colonel James McDowell).

Negro Derry - Servant - Lieutenant Colonel Thomas Hinds' Cavalry Battalion, Mississippi Militia.

Negro Derry - Servant - Delcouet's Regiment, Louisiana Militia (Lieutenant Colonel Philip Caldwell).

Negro Gabriel - Servant - 27th Regiment, Maryland Militia (Colonel Kennedy Long).

Negro George - Servant - Delcouet's Regiment, Louisiana Militia (Lieutenant Colonel Philip Caldwell).

Negro George - Servant - 57th Regiment, Virginia Militia (Colonel Armistead J. Mason).

Negro George - Waiter - 1st Regiment, West Tennessee Militia (Colonel William Metcalfe).

Negro Green - Servant - Lieutenant Colonel Thomas Hinds' Cavalry Battalion, Mississippi Militia.

Black Regulars and Militiamen in the War of 1812

Negro Guy - Servant - 41st Regiment, Virginia Militia (Lieutenant Colonel Vincent Bramham).

Negro Harry - Servant - 40th Regiment, Maryland Militia (Lieutenant Colonel Andrew Turner).

Negro Harry - Waiter - 42nd Regiment, Maryland Militia (Lieutenant Colonel William Smith).

Negro Henry - Servant - 57th Regiment, Virginia Militia (Colonel Armistead J. Mason).

Negro Henry - Private - 27th Regiment, Maryland Militia (Colonel Kennedy Long).

Negro Jack - Waiter - 42nd Regiment, Maryland Militia (Lieutenant Colonel William Smith).

Negro Jack - Private servant - 1st Regiment, West Tennessee Militia (Colonel William Metcalfe).

Negro Jack - Servant - 7th Cavalry Regiment, Maryland Militia (Lieutenant Colonel John Streett).

Negro James - Servant - 57th Regiment, Virginia Militia (Colonel Armistead J. Mason).

Negro James - Servant - 39th Regiment, Virginia Militia.

Negro James - Servant - 40th Regiment, Maryland Militia (Lieutenant Colonel Andrew Turner).

Negro Jesse - Private - 27th Regiment, Maryland Militia (Colonel Kennedy Long).

Negro Leeds - Waiter - 3rd Regiment, West Tennessee Militia (Colonel James Roulston).

Negro London - Private servant - 1st Regiment, West Tennessee Militia (Colonel William Metcalfe).

Negro Michael - Servant - 27th Regiment, Maryland Militia (Colonel Kennedy Long).

Negro Nace - Servant - 27th Regiment, Maryland Militia (Colonel Kennedy Long).

Negro Nat - Waiter - 42nd Regiment, Maryland Militia (Lieutenant Colonel William Smith).

Negro Nathan - Servant - 32nd Regiment, Maryland Militia (Colonel Thomas Hood).

Negro Natt - Servant - 27th Regiment, Maryland Militia (Colonel Kennedy Long).

Negro Nedd - Servant - 1st Regiment, Maryland Militia (Colonel John Ragan).

Negro Perry - Servant - 49th Regiment, Maryland Militia (Lieutenant Colonel Thomas W. Veazey).

Negro Perry - Servant - Delcouet's Regiment, Louisiana Militia (Lieutenant Colonel Philip Caldwell).

Negro Perry - Waiter - 42nd Regiment, Maryland Militia (Lieutenant Colonel William Smith).

Negro Primas - Drummer - 2nd Regiment, Maryland Militia.

Negro Prince - Waiter - 2nd Regiment, Georgia Militia (Colonel Jett Thomas).

Negro Richard - Servant - 40th Regiment, Maryland Militia (Lieutenant Colonel Andrew Turner).

The Militiamen

Negro Richard - Seaman - Brigadier General Nathaniel Watson's Division, Pennsylvania Militia.

Negro Robert - Servant - 27th Regiment, Maryland Militia (Colonel Kennedy Long).

Negro Simon - Servant - 2nd Regiment, Illinois Militia.

Negro Solomon - Servant - 27th Regiment, Maryland Militia (Colonel Kennedy Long).

Negro Tom - Waiter - 42nd Regiment, Maryland Militia (Lieutenant Colonel William Smith).

Negro Tom - Servant - 38th Regiment, Maryland Militia (Lieutenant Colonel Thomas Wright).

Negro Tom - Servant - 27th Regiment, Maryland Militia (Colonel Kennedy Long).

Negro Tom - Servant - 1st Regiment, Maryland Militia (Colonel John Ragan).

Negro Tom - Servant - 27th Regiment, Maryland Militia (Colonel Kennedy Long).

Negro Toney - Waiter - Lieutenant Colonel David Neilson's Detachment, Mississippi Militia.

Negro Wassil - Waiter - 38th Regiment, Maryland Militia (Lieutenant Colonel Thomas Wright).

Ninville, Pierre - Private - Major Louis D'Aquin's 2nd Battalion, Louisiana Militia.

Noye, Narcisse - Sergeant - Lieutenant Colonel Michael Fortier's 1st Battalion, Louisiana Militia.

Olivert, Pierre - Private - Lieutenant Colonel Michael Fortier's 1st Battalion, Louisiana Militia.

Olivier, Esope - Private - Major Louis D'Aquin's 2nd Battalion, Louisiana Militia.

Opteque, Pierre - Private - Major Louis D'Aquin's 2nd Battalion, Louisiana Militia.

Orver, Michel - Private - Major Louis D'Aquin's 2nd Battalion, Louisiana Militia.

Pacaud, Francis - First Lieutenant - Lieutenant Colonel Michael Fortier's 1st Battalion, Louisiana Militia.

Parent, Pierre - Sergeant - Lieutenant Colonel Michael Fortier's 1st Battalion, Louisiana Militia.

Pascal, Frederic - Private - Major Louis D'Aquin's 2nd Battalion, Louisiana Militia.

Paul, Henry - Musician - Lieutenant Colonel Michael Fortier's 1st Battalion, Louisiana Militia.

Paule, Charles - Private - Lieutenant Colonel Michael Fortier's 1st Battalion, Louisiana Militia.

Paule, Joseph - Sergeant - Lieutenant Colonel Michael Fortier's 1st Battalion, Louisiana Militia.

Pechon, Jean Baptiste - Private - Lieutenant Colonel Michael Fortier's 1st Battalion, Louisiana Militia.

Peconnet, Jh. - Private - Major Louis D'Aquin's 2nd Battalion, Louisiana Militia.

Peraux, Firman - Private - Lieutenant Colonel Michael Fortier's 1st Battalion, Louisiana Militia.

Black Regulars and Militiamen in the War of 1812

Petit, Louis - Corporal - Major Louis D'Aquin's 2nd Battalion, Louisiana Militia.

Petit, Maurice - Private - Lieutenant Colonel Michael Fortier's 1st Battalion, Louisiana Militia.

Philibert, Jean - Private - Major Louis D'Aquin's 2nd Battalion, Louisiana Militia.

Piconnet, Jh. - Private - Major Louis D'Aquin's 2nd Battalion, Louisiana Militia.

Piernas, Louis - Private - Lieutenant Colonel Michael Fortier's 1st Battalion, Louisiana Militia.

Pierre, Baptiste - Private - Lieutenant Colonel Michael Fortier's 1st Battalion, Louisiana Militia.

Pierre, Charles - Private - Lieutenant Colonel Michael Fortier's 1st Battalion, Louisiana Militia.

Pierre, Francois - Private - Lieutenant Colonel Michael Fortier's 1st Battalion, Louisiana Militia.

Pierre, Jean - Private - Major Louis D'Aquin's 2nd Battalion, Louisiana Militia.

Pierre, Manuel Jean - Corporal - Lieutenant Colonel Michael Fortier's 1st Battalion, Louisiana Militia.

Pierre, Norbert - Private - Lieutenant Colonel Michael Fortier's 1st Battalion, Louisiana Militia.

Pierre, Paul - Private - Lieutenant Colonel Michael Fortier's 1st Battalion, Louisiana Militia.

Pierre, Sanon - Private - Lieutenant Colonel Michael Fortier's 1st Battalion, Louisiana Militia.

Pierre, Silvin - Private - Lieutenant Colonel Michael Fortier's 1st Battalion, Louisiana Militia.

Pinean, Jean - Private - Major Louis D'Aquin's 2nd Battalion, Louisiana Militia.

Pomet, Garcon - Private - Lieutenant Colonel Michael Fortier's 1st Battalion, Louisiana Militia.

Pomett, Lindor - Private - Lieutenant Colonel Michael Fortier's 1st Battalion, Louisiana Militia.

Ponton, Joachim - Private - Lieutenant Colonel Michael Fortier's 1st Battalion, Louisiana Militia.

Popplus, Barytholemy - Third Lieutenant - Lieutenant Colonel Michael Fortier's 1st Battalion, Louisiana Militia.

Populus, Carlos - Private - Lieutenant Colonel Michael Fortier's 1st Battalion, Louisiana Militia.

Populus, Charles - Sergeant - Lieutenant Colonel Michael Fortier's 1st Battalion, Louisiana Militia.

Populus, Felix - Corporal - Lieutenant Colonel Michael Fortier's 1st Battalion, Louisiana Militia.

Populus, Honore - Private - Lieutenant Colonel Michael Fortier's 1st Battalion, Louisiana Militia.

Populus, Jean Baptiste - Corporal - Lieutenant Colonel Michael Fortier's 1st Battalion, Louisiana Militia.

Populus, Joachim - Private - Lieutenant Colonel Michael Fortier's 1st Battalion, Louisiana Militia.

Populus, Maurice - First Lieutenant - Lieutenant Colonel Michael Fortier's 1st Battalion, Louisiana

Militia.

Populus, Phillipe - Private - Lieutenant Colonel Michael Fortier's 1st Battalion, Louisiana Militia.

Populus, Vincent - Major - Lieutenant Colonel Michael Fortier's 1st Battalion, Louisiana Militia.

Poree, Charles - Captain - Lieutenant Colonel Michael Fortier's 1st Battalion, Louisiana Militia.

Poree, Francois - First Lieutenant - Lieutenant Colonel Michael Fortier's 1st Battalion, Louisiana Militia.

Postique, Pierre - Corporal - Lieutenant Colonel Michael Fortier's 1st Battalion, Louisiana Militia.

Pouyesse, Louis - Sergeant - Lieutenant Colonel Michael Fortier's 1st Battalion, Louisiana Militia.

Prade, Zenon - Private - Lieutenant Colonel Michael Fortier's 1st Battalion, Louisiana Militia.

Prado, Sebastian - Private - Lieutenant Colonel Michael Fortier's 1st Battalion, Louisiana Militia.

Prados, Pierre - Private - Lieutenant Colonel Michael Fortier's 1st Battalion, Louisiana Militia.

Prevot, Honore - Private - Lieutenant Colonel Michael Fortier's 1st Battalion, Louisiana Militia.

Quessart, J. - Sergeant Major - Lieutenant Colonel Michael Fortier's 1st Battalion, Louisiana Militia.

Raby, Antoine - Private - Lieutenant Colonel Michael Fortier's 1st Battalion, Louisiana Militia.

Raimond, Honore - Private - Lieutenant Colonel Michael Fortier's 1st Battalion, Louisiana Militia.

Ramond, Joseph - Private - Lieutenant Colonel Michael Fortier's 1st Battalion, Louisiana Militia.

Raphael, Bazile - Private - Major Louis D'Aquin's 2nd Battalion, Louisiana Militia.

Raphael, Fils - Private - Lieutenant Colonel Michael Fortier's 1st Battalion, Louisiana Militia.

Raphael, Pierre - Corporal - Lieutenant Colonel Michael Fortier's 1st Battalion, Louisiana Militia.

Raquet, Honore - Private - Lieutenant Colonel Michael Fortier's 1st Battalion, Louisiana Militia.

Raymond, Honore - Private - Lieutenant Colonel Michael Fortier's 1st Battalion, Louisiana Militia.

Raynes, Joseph - Corporal - Lieutenant Colonel Michael Fortier's 1st Battalion, Louisiana Militia.

Reau, Garcon - Private - Lieutenant Colonel Michael Fortier's 1st Battalion, Louisiana Militia.

Reaux, Silveste - Private - Lieutenant Colonel Michael Fortier's 1st Battalion, Louisiana Militia.

Redouin, Jaques - Private - Major Louis D'Aquin's 2nd Battalion, Louisiana Militia.

Remy, Antoine - Private - Major Louis D'Aquin's 2nd Battalion, Louisiana Militia.

Resimond, Ninniere - Private - Lieutenant Colonel Michael Fortier's 1st Battalion, Louisiana Militia.

Black Regulars and Militiamen in the War of 1812

Reynes, Joseph - Corporal - Lieutenant Colonel Michael Fortier's 1st Battalion, Louisiana Militia.

Ribon, Mannuelle - Private - Major Louis D'Aquin's 2nd Battalion, Louisiana Militia.

Riboul, Appolonaire - Private - Lieutenant Colonel Michael Fortier's 1st Battalion, Louisiana Militia.

Richard, John - Private - Lieutenant Colonel Michael Fortier's 1st Battalion, Louisiana Militia.

Rieux, Honotr - Private - Lieutenant Colonel Michael Fortier's 1st Battalion, Louisiana Militia.

Rivarosse, Mathierin - Private - Lieutenant Colonel Michael Fortier's 1st Battalion, Louisiana Militia.

Robert, Angel - Private - Major Louis D'Aquin's 2nd Battalion, Louisiana Militia.

Robert, Fife - Private - Major Louis D'Aquin's 2nd Battalion, Louisiana Militia.

Robert, Jacques - Private - Lieutenant Colonel Michael Fortier's 1st Battalion, Louisiana Militia.

Robert, Severin - Sergeant - Lieutenant Colonel Michael Fortier's 1st Battalion, Louisiana Militia.

Robertson, Cato - Servant - 1st Regiment, New York Militia (Lieutenant Colonel Beekman M. Vanbenren).

Robin, Norbert - Private - Lieutenant Colonel Michael Fortier's 1st Battalion, Louisiana Militia.

Roches, Charles - Corporal - Lieutenant Colonel Michael Fortier's 1st Battalion, Louisiana Militia.

Rochon, Hilaire - Private - Lieutenant Colonel Michael Fortier's 1st Battalion, Louisiana Militia.

Rodenay, Pierre - Private - Major Louis D'Aquin's 2nd Battalion, Louisiana Militia.

Roland, Baptiste - Private - Lieutenant Colonel Michael Fortier's 1st Battalion, Louisiana Militia.

Roland, Guillaume - Private - Major Louis D'Aquin's 2nd Battalion, Louisiana Militia.

Rolet, Felix - Private - Major Louis D'Aquin's 2nd Battalion, Louisiana Militia.

Romagnan, Francois - Private - Lieutenant Colonel Michael Fortier's 1st Battalion, Louisiana Militia.

Romin, Casemure - Corporal - Major Louis D'Aquin's 2nd Battalion, Louisiana Militia.

Roque, Elise - Private - Lieutenant Colonel Michael Fortier's 1st Battalion, Louisiana Militia.

Roquigne, Jean Baptiste - Private - Lieutenant Colonel Michael Fortier's 1st Battalion, Louisiana Militia.

Rosemond, Miniere - Private - Lieutenant Colonel Michael Fortier's 1st Battalion, Louisiana Militia.

Rosemond, Vincent - Private - Lieutenant Colonel Michael Fortier's 1st Battalion, Louisiana Militia.

Rosson, Charles - Private - Lieutenant Colonel Michael Fortier's 1st Battalion, Louisiana Militia.

Rouland, Rene - Corporal - Major Louis D'Aquin's 2nd Battalion, Louisiana Militia.

The Militiamen

Roulette, Bonhomme - Private - Major Louis D'Aquin's 2nd Battalion, Louisiana Militia.

Roussau, Jean - Private - Lieutenant Colonel Michael Fortier's 1st Battalion, Louisiana Militia.

Roussaux, Pierre - Private - Lieutenant Colonel Michael Fortier's 1st Battalion, Louisiana Militia.

Roussere, Baptiste - Corporal - Lieutenant Colonel Michael Fortier's 1st Battalion, Louisiana Militia.

Roussere, Manuel - Private - Lieutenant Colonel Michael Fortier's 1st Battalion, Louisiana Militia.

Rouzant, Jacques - Sergeant - Lieutenant Colonel Michael Fortier's 1st Battalion, Louisiana Militia.

Rouzier, Berlin - Captain - Major Louis D'Aquin's 2nd Battalion, Louisiana Militia.

Rynes, Joseph - Corporal - Lieutenant Colonel Michael Fortier's 1st Battalion, Louisiana Militia.

Sabagere, Pierre - Private - Lieutenant Colonel Michael Fortier's 1st Battalion, Louisiana Militia.

Saintraille, F. - Private - Major Louis D'Aquin's 2nd Battalion, Louisiana Militia.

Sandos, Isidor - Private - Lieutenant Colonel Michael Fortier's 1st Battalion, Louisiana Militia.

Sarasin, Louis - Private - Major Louis D'Aquin's 2nd Battalion, Louisiana Militia.

Sarazin, Joseph - Sergeant - Major Louis D'Aquin's 2nd Battalion, Louisiana Militia.

Sarestle, Baptiste - Private - Lieutenant Colonel Michael Fortier's 1st Battalion, Louisiana Militia.

Sauvages, Charles - Private - Lieutenant Colonel Michael Fortier's 1st Battalion, Louisiana Militia.

Savarie, Belton - Sergeant - Major Louis D'Aquin's 2nd Battalion, Louisiana Militia.

Savary, Joseph - Major - Major Louis D'Aquin's 2nd Battalion, Louisiana Militia.

Sejour, Louis - Quartermaster Sergeant - Major Louis D'Aquin's 2nd Battalion, Louisiana Militia.

Servian, Paul - Corporal - Major Louis D'Aquin's 2nd Battalion, Louisiana Militia.

Silvest, Joseph - Corporal - Lieutenant Colonel Michael Fortier's 1st Battalion, Louisiana Militia.

Simon, Louis - Captain - Lieutenant Colonel Michael Fortier's 1st Battalion, Louisiana Militia.

Smith, Richard - Private - Lieutenant Colonel Michael Fortier's 1st Battalion, Louisiana Militia.

Smith, Stephen - Black waiter - 3rd Brigade, New York Militia (Brigadier General Jonas Mapes).

St. Amant, Ss. - Private - Lieutenant Colonel Michael Fortier's 1st Battalion, Louisiana Militia.

St. Amant, Voltaire - Private - Lieutenant Colonel Michael Fortier's 1st Battalion, Louisiana Militia.

St. Anaille, F. - Private - Major Louis D'Aquin's 2nd Battalion, Louisiana Militia.

Black Regulars and Militiamen in the War of 1812

St. Aubin, Montagne - Sergeant - Major Louis D'Aquin's 2nd Battalion, Louisiana Militia.

St. Martin, S. - Private - Lieutenant Colonel Michael Fortier's 1st Battalion, Louisiana Militia.

Stanisclas, Victor - Private - Major Louis D'Aquin's 2nd Battalion, Louisiana Militia.

Stanislas, Victor - Private - Major Louis D'Aquin's 2nd Battalion, Louisiana Militia.

Stephen, William - Private - Lieutenant Colonel Michael Fortier's 1st Battalion, Louisiana Militia.

Stibine, William - Private - Lieutenant Colonel Michael Fortier's 1st Battalion, Louisiana Militia.

Tabutean, Pierre - Private - Major Louis D'Aquin's 2nd Battalion, Louisiana Militia.

Taillot, Henry - Private - Major Louis D'Aquin's 2nd Battalion, Louisiana Militia.

Talabert, Cadet - Corporal - Major Louis D'Aquin's 2nd Battalion, Louisiana Militia.

Tardos, Etienne - Private - Major Louis D'Aquin's 2nd Battalion, Louisiana Militia.

Telier, Lowis - Private - Major Louis D'Aquin's 2nd Battalion, Louisiana Militia.

Tellfain, Louis - Private - Major Louis D'Aquin's 2nd Battalion, Louisiana Militia.

Ternoir, Jean - Captain - Lieutenant Colonel Michael Fortier's 1st Battalion, Louisiana Militia.

Theard, Joseph - Private - Lieutenant Colonel Michael Fortier's 1st Battalion, Louisiana Militia.

Theen, Lucien - Private - Major Louis D'Aquin's 2nd Battalion, Louisiana Militia.

Theodor, Honore - Private - Lieutenant Colonel Michael Fortier's 1st Battalion, Louisiana Militia.

Thiery, Bazille - Private - Lieutenant Colonel Michael Fortier's 1st Battalion, Louisiana Militia.

Thomas, Antoine - Private - Lieutenant Colonel Michael Fortier's 1st Battalion, Louisiana Militia.

Thomas, James - Private - Lieutenant Colonel Michael Fortier's 1st Battalion, Louisiana Militia.

Thomas, Monplaiser - Sergeant - Major Louis D'Aquin's 2nd Battalion, Louisiana Militia.

Toraille, Jean - Private - Major Louis D'Aquin's 2nd Battalion, Louisiana Militia.

Travert, Frans - Private - Major Louis D'Aquin's 2nd Battalion, Louisiana Militia.

Trebino, Paul - Corporal - Lieutenant Colonel Michael Fortier's 1st Battalion, Louisiana Militia.

Trebino, Raimond - Private - Lieutenant Colonel Michael Fortier's 1st Battalion, Louisiana Militia.

Treme, Emile - Musician - Lieutenant Colonel Michael Fortier's 1st Battalion, Louisiana Militia.

Treme, Felix - Musician - Lieutenant Colonel Michael Fortier's 1st Battalion, Louisiana Militia.

The Militiamen

Ursin, Andre - Private - Major Louis D'Aquin's 2nd Battalion, Louisiana Militia.

Valentine, Ursin - Private - Lieutenant Colonel Michael Fortier's 1st Battalion, Louisiana Militia.

Valiere, Antoine - Private - Lieutenant Colonel Michael Fortier's 1st Battalion, Louisiana Militia.

Valiere, Joseph - Private - Lieutenant Colonel Michael Fortier's 1st Battalion, Louisiana Militia.

Valiere, Ls. - Private - Lieutenant Colonel Michael Fortier's 1st Battalion, Louisiana Militia.

Valingtine, Samuel - Private - Lieutenant Colonel Michael Fortier's 1st Battalion, Louisiana Militia.

Vallentine, Urcins - Private - Lieutenant Colonel Michael Fortier's 1st Battalion, Louisiana Militia.

Vallier, Baptiste - Corporal - Lieutenant Colonel Michael Fortier's 1st Battalion, Louisiana Militia.

Vallier, Brunaux - Private - Lieutenant Colonel Michael Fortier's 1st Battalion, Louisiana Militia.

Vallier, Joseph - Private - Lieutenant Colonel Michael Fortier's 1st Battalion, Louisiana Militia.

Vallier, Louis - Private - Lieutenant Colonel Michael Fortier's 1st Battalion, Louisiana Militia.

Valliere, Ss - Private - Lieutenant Colonel Michael Fortier's 1st Battalion, Louisiana Militia.

Ventourind, Raymond - Musician - Lieutenant Colonel Michael Fortier's 1st Battalion, Louisiana Militia.

Verdery, Francois - Private - Major Louis D'Aquin's 2nd Battalion, Louisiana Militia.

Vial, Antoine - Corporal - Major Louis D'Aquin's 2nd Battalion, Louisiana Militia.

Victor, Charles - Private - Major Louis D'Aquin's 2nd Battalion, Louisiana Militia.

Victor, Zenon - Private - Lieutenant Colonel Michael Fortier's 1st Battalion, Louisiana Militia.

Vilstz, Charles - Private - Lieutenant Colonel Michael Fortier's 1st Battalion, Louisiana Militia.

Vivant, Charles - First Lieutenant - Lieutenant Colonel Michael Fortier's 1st Battalion, Louisiana Militia.

Voisin, Terence - Private - Lieutenant Colonel Michael Fortier's 1st Battalion, Louisiana Militia.

Warnis, Joseph - Private - Lieutenant Colonel Michael Fortier's 1st Battalion, Louisiana Militia.

Warnisse, Joseph - Private - Lieutenant Colonel Michael Fortier's 1st Battalion, Louisiana Militia.

Washington, George - Drummer - Colonel Robert Rose's Regiment, Virginia Militia - Pension: SO-29898 – List as "Colored."

Wiltz, Bastien - Private - Lieutenant Colonel Michael Fortier's 1st Battalion, Louisiana Militia.

Wiltz, Sambert - Private - Lieutenant Colonel Michael Fortier's 1st Battalion, Louisiana Militia.

Ybare, Desire - Private - Major Louis D'Aquin's 2nd Battalion, Louisiana Militia.

The Bibliography

Adjutant and Inspector General's Office, *Military Laws and Rules and Regulations for the Army of the United States*, September 1816, (E. De Krafft, Printer: Washington, DC).

Clark, Byron N., *A List of Pensioners of the War of 1812*, (Research Publications Company: Burlington and Boston, 1904).

Drum, Richard C. (Brigadier General), *Adjutant General's Department*, Subject Index of the General Orders of the War Department from January 1, 1809 to December 31, 1860.

General Entry Book of American Prisoners of War ledger of the British Admiralty made by the Public Record Office in London, Great Britain (ADM 103 / 167, 168 and 362).

Heitman, Francis B., *Historical Register and Dictionary of the United States Army From Its Organization, September 29, 1789, to March 2, 1903*, Volume I, (Genealogical Publishing Company, Baltimore, Maryland: 1994).

Irving, L. Homfray, *Officers of the British Forces in Canada during the War of 1812*, (Welland Tribune Printers, 1908).

Miscellaneous Lists and Records of the British Admiralty made by the Public Record Office in London, Great Britain (ADM 103 / 465, part 2).

Moebs, Thomas Truxtun, *Black Soldiers – Black Sailors – Black Ink: Research Guide of African-Americans in U.S. Military History, 1512-1900*, (Moebs Publishing Co.: Chesapeake Bay, VA 1994).

Montgomery, Thomas Lynch, *Pennsylvania Archives*, Sixth Series, volumes 7 through 10, (Harrisburg Publishing Company, State Printers: Harrisburg, PA 1907), War of 1812-1814.

National Archives and Records Administration, *Index to the Compiled Military Service Records for the Volunteer Soldiers Who Served During the War of 1812*, (Washington, D.C.: National Archives and Records Administration), M602.

National Park Service, U.S. Department of the Interior, *39th Infantry Muster Roll*, May 1814, Battle of Horseshoe Bend, http://www.nps.gov/hobe/upload/39infantry.pdf.

Official Correspondence with the Department of War relative to the Military Operations of the American Army under the Command of Major General Izard of the Northern Frontier of the United States in the Years 1814 and 1815, (William Fry, Printer: Philadelphia, 1816).

Peters, Richard, *The Public Statutes at Large of the United States of America*, Volumes I and II, (Charles C. Little and James Brown: Boston, MA 1845).

Records of Officers and Men of New Jersey in Wars 1791-1815, (Adjutant-General's Office: Trenton, NY 1909), part V, War with Great Britain 1812-1815.

Records Relating to War of 1812 Prisoners of War, 1812; (Washington, DC: National Archives Microfilm Publication M2019); Records of the Adjutant General's Office, 1780's-1917; Record Group 94, compiled by Clair Prechtel-Kluskens.

Register of Enlistments in the U.S. Army, 1798-1914; (Washington, DC: National Archives Microfilm Publication M233, 81 rolls); Records of the Adjutant General's Office, 1780's-1917, Record Group 94.

Sander, George P., *The Statues at Large, Treaties and Proclamations of the United States of America*, Volume XII, (Little, Brown and Company: Boston, MA 1863).

Stagg, J.C.A., *Enlisted Men in the United States Army, 1812-1815: A Preliminary Survey, William and Mary Quarterly,* Third Series, Volume XLIII, Number 4, October 1986, pages 615-645.

United States. Bureau of Land Management, General Land Office Records. Automated Records Project; *Federal Land Patents*, State Volumes. http://www.glorecords.blm.gov/. Springfield, Virginia: Bureau of Land Management, Eastern States, 2007.

War Department, Rules and Regulations Respecting the Recruiting Service, April 5, 1799, Article III.

War of 1812 Military Bounty Land Warrants, 1815-1858; (Washington, DC: National Archives Microfilm Publication M848, 14 rolls); Records of the Bureau of Land Management, Record Group 49.

War of 1812 Pension Applications; (Washington D.C.: National Archives, NARA Microfilm Publication M313, 102 rolls), Records of the Department of Veterans Affairs, Record Group Number 15.

Wilkes, Laura E., *Missing Pages in American History: Revealing the Service of Negroes in the Early Wars in the United States of America, 1641-1815*, (Press of R. L. Pendleton: Washington, DC, 1919).

Williams, George W., *History of the Negro Race in America from 1619 to 1880*, (G. P. Putnam's Sons: New York, 1883), volume II.

Wilson, Joseph T., *The Black Phalanx: A History of the Negro Soldiers of the United States in the Wars of 1775-1812, 1861-1865*, (American Publishing Company: Hartford, CT, 1890).

About the Author

ERIC E. JOHNSON serves as the archivist general for the General Society of the War of 1812 and as the registrar/genealogist for the Society of the War of 1812 in the State of Ohio. He is a trustee for the Ohio Genealogical Society and is a member of the National Society Sons of the American Revolution, the Swedish Colonial Society and the Company of Military Historians. He is a retired lieutenant colonel in the United States Air Force.

THE SOCIETY OF THE WAR OF 1812 IN THE STATE OF OHIO was formed on 8 January 1895 and the society is a chapter of the General Society of the War of 1812. The purpose of this society is to perpetuate the memories of the participants of the War of 1812; to collect, secure, and preserve any rolls, records, books, documents, or artifacts relating to the period of the War of 1812; and to encourage research and publications of the history of the patriots and landmarks of the era of the War of 1812.